"Teach Them to Love One Another"

"Teach Them to Love One Another"

Terry W. Treseder

BOOKCRAFT
Salt Lake City, Utah

Library of Congress Catalog Card Number: 84-73289
ISBN 0-88494-555-3

First Printing, 1985

Printed in the United States of America

And ye will not suffer your children that they go hungry, or naked; neither will ye suffer that they transgress the laws of God, and fight and quarrel one with another, . . .

But ye will teach them to walk in the ways of truth and soberness; ye will teach them to love one another, and to serve one another.

—Mosiah 4:14–15

Contents

1

Children Need Love from Each Other

Have you ever taught a home evening or Primary lesson and felt as if you were shouting into a seventy-mile-per-hour hurricane—as if the words were being shoved back into your throat? That's how I feel when I give a lesson on the topic "Love One Another" and I hear the following among the children: "Yuk—I don't want to sit by you!" "I don't want to sit by you either!" "Zit-face!" "Nerd!" "You think you're so smart!" "Yeah, I'm smart enough to know how dumb you are!" Parents have told me similar stories about family home evenings: "Sometimes I feel like we're doing more harm than good. They start off peacefully watching TV. We bring them together for family time—you know, for love and togetherness—and they end up fighting World War III in our living room."

How do you teach children to love one another—really love each other? This question has haunted me ever since I started teaching Primary many years ago.

My ward leaders must have been desperate: As soon as I graduated from Primary I was called to be a Primary teacher. Having a twelve-year-old teacher must have been interesting for ten-year-old students.

Being a twelve-year-old teacher was even more intriguing. Every time I went to the library to pick up my visual aids, a kindly sister would bend over the Dutch door and inquire sweetly, "And who is your teacher, dear?" When the secretary came to pick up the roll, she would invariably look around the room with a mixture of puzzlement and irritation. "Now, where is your teacher this time?" We had a lot of fun in that class. We could talk about lessons girl to girl. We laughed a great deal.

I've never been out of the Primary since. Even when I attended college, they had a Primary class waiting for me during the summer. It got to be a joke with my friends: "How many kids do you have now?" Over the years I've had the joy of associating with children of all ages and personalities, from three to twelve, from smart to "slow," from quiet to active. I've learned a lot growing up as a Primary teacher. Being a child myself when I started, I had a perspective that was quite different from an adult's. I had the advantage of knowing firsthand what was important to children. I knew what hurt and what brought joy. I saw the little things that older people might have missed—things that were said or done to inflict pain or bring comfort.

I also knew what most teachers and parents feel instinctively—that love is the most effective tool for teaching any principle. Without it, a child has no interest or desire to learn. We all know how important it is to develop relationships with our children. Volumes of literature and aids help adults feel and express love for the little ones in their lives. But there is another source of love that is often forgotten by the adult world. I never had a chance to forget it. I grew up dealing with it in my personal life, while at the same time observing it with empathetic eyes in the classroom. The older the children, the more important this source of love becomes. Children need love from each other.

So the question arose and grew more important

with each passing year: How do you teach children to love each other? Until I left for college I could never find a satisfactory answer to that challenge. I tried all sorts of crazy experiments—lectures, spotlights, parties, talent shows, stories, songs. I even taught a group of children how to dance the polka, figuring that a group who dance together love together. Unfortunately, one boy never got the hang of it, so he got hanged by his peers. Instead of, "Boy, that was fun! We're great together!" I heard, "Stupid nitwit! Can't you do anything without falling on your face!"

Thanks to the law of averages, I did have some successes. If you try hard enough, long enough, you will eventually master anything. At the rate I was going, however, it would have taken fifty years, fifty classes, and approximately three hundred juvenile casualties to put together *the formula* for confident success.

Happily for me, and for the unborn spirits fated to enter my classroom, I discovered something very close to this formula. I would like to share what I discovered with you so that you can use it as a teacher or as a parent. The games and activities in this book are based on sound interpersonal principles and childhood personalities. And if you are a teacher, I can guarantee you pleasant surprises. Since stumbling onto this formula I have experienced the great joy of watching children "come together" in every class I have taught during the past seven years. If you are a parent, you will probably experience even more success than I ever did as a teacher. Why? Research throughout the country has proven over and over again that any parent can teach his child anything better than the best teacher or program available.

It all started because I couldn't afford to go to college without a scholarship. The only scholarship I could get was in public speaking. To keep the scholarship I had to major in some field of communication. I tried all the glamorous courses first—journalism,

broadcasting, forensics. Then one semester I saun-
tered into a dull-sounding class called "Small Group
Communication."

It turned out to be the most exciting semester in
my life. Many times during that course the light bulb
would turn on, electric currents would shoot up, and I
had the uncontrollable urge to jump up and shout with
ecstasy: "That's right! It fits! My prayers have been
answered!" As soon as the class period was over, I'd
bolt out of that room, dash to my cubicle, and madly
write down the ideas that were bursting like fire-
crackers out of my head. "Just wait until I try this on
my next Primary class." I changed my major to Interpersonal Communication. Now, years after earning
my degree, I am still fascinated by this area of research. Better yet, I have never had a failure since
then. The system works for any group of children, no
matter how terrible their relationships are.

The field of interpersonal communication is rela-
tively new, about twenty-five years in the making; it is
an infant compared to its ancient ancestor, psychol-
ogy. My particular area of specialization—group
dynamics—is even ten years newer. Whereas psychol-
ogy deals mostly with the inner workings of troubled
or abnormal people, interpersonal communication
studies interactions between normal people. It dissects
what people say and do to each other, analyzes the
problems that occur, and seeks remedies to those
problems. Since graduates usually look for some way
to earn a living, this fledgling field had to find salary-
paying sponsors to keep the program alive. It was the
business world that embraced interpersonal consultants most enthusiastically. Companies discovered
that when their employees were trained to get along
with each other and with their clients, turnover went
down and morale, productivity, and profits went up.

These marvelous results are obtained in spite of the
negative attitudes most employees have about training seminars and the long years of bad habits and

political back stabbing that may plague a corporation. How do consultants do it? To oversimplify, they use two basic strategies in every training session. First, the trainer never picks out individuals for change, but instead regards the group as a single unit to be worked on as a whole. Second, after spending a few minutes teaching an interpersonal skill, he puts the group in a "structured experience," a game or activity designed in such a way that the only way the group can achieve the goal or win the game is to practice the skill just taught. Human nature being what it is, people will do anything to win something—even try new and uncomfortable behaviors. Given enough of these exercises, employees acquire the skills in spite of themselves. The technique works. Millions of dollars are made every year by consultant firms throughout the country who send trainers out to teach executives how to work with people.

The program of study I had, then, was geared toward company employees. We were taught how to evaluate social patterns in a work group and how to run workshops that taught basic communication skills—the kind of skills every human being needs in order to experience good relationships with other people. The principles are simple. The training strategies are even simpler. Yet they are being sought by corporations, social agencies, marriage counselors, and secondary school systems. Many universities require an interpersonal communication course for their business majors.

Although everything I learned targeted adults in the workaday world, it was natural for me to translate it all to children. Will this work on my five-year-olds? How can I change this exercise so that my eight-year-olds can do it? Given the right modifications, group dynamics should apply to any group of people at any age. Don't we all need affection, respect, and recognition from other people? Any group of people can benefit from small group training: IBM employees, family members, or ten-year-olds in a Primary class. The basic principles are the same for all of us. The trick is to modify the learning strategies for a younger age. We need to adjust for reading and writing limitations, juvenile interests, lesson content (from family home evening or Primary manuals), and stages of mental and physical development.

It can be done, and with tremendous success. Having taught both adults and children, I can testify that children learn social skills four times faster than adults. Children retain what they learn for longer periods of time—and they love it. No more hit-and-miss experiments. No more casualties. There's nothing sweeter than watching the magic put love into your children. It's fun to train them—and they need the help badly.

How soon we forget the painful anxieties of childhood, the clumsy battles for identity, recognition, independence, and love! We forget so easily the savage wounds that children can inflict upon each other. Can we peel back the soft flannel coverings of our memories and reenter the fearful world we had to face once upon a time?

If we were unlucky enough to be "different" somehow—maybe we had braces, old clothes, a lisp, warts, pimples, or a "funny" name—we suffered excruciating pain from cutting nicknames, whispered giggles, or ostracism from birthday parties and baseball teams. If we were the "runt" we hardly ever had a chance to take charge or be taken seriously. If we managed to fit in, we worried about staying in, afraid to say or do anything that might be unpopular. We worried about what to wear, what and whom to like, what to hate, whom to play with. We had to keep tuned into what everyone else thought and swing with the crowd. If we were Top Dog we spent our time defending our position; picking fads, trends, and attitudes that everyone else would accept; playing our role as joker, dictator, or perfect model under any and all circumstances. We might have felt threatened by others who might take our place.

A few of us enjoyed periods of the idyllic childhood bliss we often dream about. If so, we were in a rare category. According to research, 60 percent of the children in America feel uncomfortable with each other. Because of the fluidity of children's behavior, the 40 percent of self-confident children are rarely the same ones at any given time. If we push our recollective powers hard enough, I'll bet we could all remember vividly the full range of uncomfortable struggles with rejection, anxiety, and defense.

These feelings are not healthy. They take energy away from learning, caring, and maturing. Extensive research in public schools correlates peer anxiety with low grades, delinquency, and destructive competition (excessive competition that makes children unable to cooperate in group projects). These studies also document the climbing importance of other children on a youngster's self-esteem as he grows older. This means that Mom, Dad, and teachers become more and more impotent to help the young people they care about, left to watch helplessly as children make or destroy each other. We don't need statistics to know that many children abandon the gospel when they can't find peer friendship at home or at church.

Forming social groups is a complicated business. Without guidance, the process often leaves casualties. Some child groups are productive and supportive for individual growth, but most end up with a pecking order and oppressive rules that hurt everyone.

The Outcast

The most obvious victim in a typical child group is the one who gets picked on—the outcast. We've all seen bright, eager spirits wilt, cringe, or blaze into violence under the pain of rejection. In families, it is nearly always the younger children who get emotionally beaten up every day. Some of these flayed personalities tear at the heartstrings. How we long to hold these outcasts and love them! And we do. We try to comfort them by telling them that their parents and God and others love them. Yet these assurances cannot eradicate the emotional, intellectual, and spiritual damage that occurs when a child gets nothing but "F's" from other children. Dad can keep telling Melanie, "You're beautiful." Her older sister can keep saying, "You're ugly." The sad fact is, Melanie will believe she is ugly, probably for the rest of her life.

Other victims are not so lovable. They hit, argue, throw tantrums—anything to fight back. They suffer the same feelings but react differently, often locking themselves into a never-ending cycle of rejection, misbehavior, rejection. How often have we, as teachers or parents, added our chiding voices to the chorus of "Bad boy!" These are sad cases. If not helped early, such children are doomed to a lifetime of unhappy relationships, because they turn away people who would ordinarily accept them.

Think back to a time in your childhood when you were the outcast. How did it feel? How do you feel about it now, even after all these years? I remember going to a new school right after a serious car accident. I had a bad limp. The other little girls made fun of everything I did—the way I limped, the way I sang, the way I dressed. When they refused to let me play "foursquare" I started beating everybody up. Maybe I didn't walk right, but I certainly could throw my fists! Did I take malicious delight in tearing Suzy's hair out? Of course not. I was hurt and frustrated. Fortunately, we lived there for only three months or I probably would have grown up to be a low rider in Hell's Angels. The interesting thing about this episode is that the adults concentrated on *me*, on helping Terry fit in. No one ever stopped to think that if the other little girls had been nicer there never would have been a problem in the first place.

The Ruling Monarch

Outcasts are not the only victims of childhood groups. In fact, the well-liked leader stands to lose the most in these early social games. As the saying goes, "Power corrupts; absolute power corrupts absolutely." We've seen what power can do to adults; imagine what it can do to inexperienced youngsters. These gregarious spirits enjoy almost godlike power over their friends. Johnny Athlete or Older Brother decides who is "in" and who is "out," what kind of behavior is acceptable, what games will be played. I'm ashamed to admit how I used my power sometimes when I enjoyed popularity. It was tempting to terrorize my peers with possible rejection. "You *don't* watch 'Batman?' Oh, brother, you are *out* of it!"

As adults, we've all seen this power at work. We hope Johnny makes his friends or siblings do "good things" like be reverent in class, do their chores, come to Primary. We've met not-so-benevolent leaders who make lesson discussions virtual graveyards or mutinies. Laying aside the obvious discomfort we adults feel, how does this kind of undisciplined power affect Johnny? Defensive leaders who lead rebellions against adults grow up to be extremely intolerant. Even when they "shape up" later, they are often still dictators in their homes and businesses, unable to accept initiative or criticism from subordinates. Their ability to give genuine love is also badly restricted, for tender affection is often viewed as a sign of weakness. Nurturing other people's strengths is a threat to an insecure power position. The "leader" becomes a microcosm of King Saul.

A common problem in families is the power struggle between two or more children who all want to be the "boss." They have the mistaken idea that only one person can be the leader, the most important figure in the family. These battles for achievement often tear family peace to shreds with continual bickering and back stabbing.

Adults traditionally love the "good" guy, the one who keeps his peers in line. But even this kind of leader is learning bad habits. He is still imposing on the free agency of his friends, rather than encouraging them to generate their own independent ideas and unique personalities. Though working on the side of Mom or Teacher, he is nevertheless a dictator. Do we want these bright young people to learn how to control their peers rather than love them? Whether they control through fear, approval, or charm, just how much love can they give to someone they keep under their thumbs?

The Savior was the supreme example of leadership. He nurtured the leadership abilities of his disciples. He allowed them to exercise their spiritual muscles, their talents, their self-confidence. He created other leaders. That is what Johnny needs to learn. He needs to learn that he won't lose anything by encouraging other children to take the lead once in a while. He needs to develop his natural ability to uplift his brothers and sisters so that he stands among equals, not subjects. And he will discover a greater happiness and peer respect for himself by giving his power away —the power will come back a hundredfold, as it did for the Savior.

These talented children are a joy to work with. They pick up proper leadership skills rapidly, if given half a chance. They can be taught the most advanced tips for organizing activities with their friends. They can experience an exciting new relationship with their brothers and sisters.

The Quaking Serf

The "in-betweeners" escape the awful pain of rejection and the corruptive lure of absolute power. Yet they also become victims of each other. In the anxiety to avoid being rejected, they often fall into two traps. The first is the urge to go along with the gang. Everyone is picking on Melanie. Cathy reasons that if she doesn't join in, she's going to be "out." She'd better pick on Melanie.

This happened to me more than once in my own childhood. There's one episode I would especially like to forget. An Indian girl in our school lived in a shack with her mother on the ragged side of town. She wore the same old clothes every day, a long Indian skirt and tattered moccasins. She and I became good friends, even though everyone else shunned her. We shared a lot of happy times together. We played in the wheat fields and caught grasshoppers in the sunflower patch.

One day the most popular girl in school invited me to her slumber party. I was ecstatic! I was anxious to make a good impression. The girls began to talk about my Indian friend. They laughed about her clothes. They talked about her "welfare" family. Did I defend my friend? Did I stand up with righteous anger and stomp out of the room? I wish I had! Instead, I added my own little cuts. I laughed, too. And I never played with that Indian girl again. I hurt another human being out of fear—I was afraid of rejection.

So, what does the quaking serf learn? He learns how to do things against his conscience. He learns how to be "tossed to and fro, and carried about with every wind" of peer pressure. This is contrary to the goals of the gospel, which are to strengthen the Saints, not weaken them. Quaking serfs are slaves to fear. They are vulnerable to other pressures that will come their way in life, pressures to do things against their better judgment. They are always anxious about what others think, which only eats up self-respect.

Another common problem "in-betweeners" have is their tendency to be inhibited when it comes to contributing ideas, feelings, and thoughts. Since they are comfortable in following their leader, they feel no need to explore their testimonies, creativity, or talents. "Let Johnny do all the work. I'll just agree and do what he tells me to do." This attitude is tough to break once it hardens in adulthood. Creative brainstorming becomes an atrophied muscle that must be painfully wrenched and worked over long periods of time. It's sad to see a fifty-year-old man unable to think of more than one way to use a pot, or one way to read a scripture. If children continue to sit in silence, or merely echo other youngsters' ideas, they will lose the ability to think independently. They become like the ancient Israelites and Nephites who clamored for a king: "Give us a king so we don't have to think!" Again, this mental laziness is contrary to God's plan, which glories free agency and intelligence, without which we would hardly be suitable for eternal progression toward godhood.

They All Need Help

Who wins in the typical child group? The point is, no one does. Every member of the group needs help. Often we adults actually compound their problems by trying to change a single element of the picture. We may, for example, try to compensate for Melanie's rejection by giving her extra attention. This invariably subjects her to more taunting as "teacher's pet" and makes her completely dependent on Mom or Teacher for affection. In a family, this approach can inflame jealousies among the other children and actually polarize them permanently.

We may try to change Melanie herself, change whatever seems to be "different" about her. We may discourage her from answering too many questions, singing so loudly, or wearing her hair in "fuddy-duddy" braids. What do we teach when we adjust a child into her group? We smother Melanie's uniqueness, teach her to be an "in-betweener." We confirm the group's power and teach other children that it pays to punish each other for breaking their arbitrary rules.

Sometimes we approach the group itself and shame them into treating Melanie with respect. I've done this many times and enjoyed limited success, perhaps because I attacked a larger segment of the problem. But Melanie may become an object of patronizing pity, rather than true friendship. She may be pressured, albeit with kindness, into conforming with everyone else and never allowed to assert leadership. By singling her out for group attention, we automatically classify her as "abnormal" in the minds of her peers. This kind of acceptance is better than nothing at all. But don't we want something better for her?

Concentrating on the outcast can backfire in weird ways. I remember a seven-year-old girl named Peggy. Her crooked braids pulled her hair back so tightly that she could never quite close her mouth over a formidable array of metal braces. Her Tinkertoy arms and legs stuck out of ill-fitting clothes and scuffed loafers. Hungry, timid eyes begged for affection. In short, she was the kind of Raggedy Ann I wanted to gather in my arms and rock. The other kids called her Metal Mouth and continually poked fun at her. I could feel the knives every time Peggy made the unfortunate mistake of being noticed.

Finally I had had enough. I gave a scorching lecture, complete with raging glare and folded arms. I blasted those children so mightily that their eyes grew into terrified saucers. What had happened to their sweet little teacher? they wondered. And I ended with the fateful words, "Now, you'd better quit picking on Peggy, *or else!*"

They did stop picking on Peggy. Then the real nightmare began. Peggy began to pick on *them.* "Teacher," she would pout, pointing at Eric, "he laughed at me." Everyone waited to see what "or else" I was going to do to Eric. And so it began. Every time Peggy complained, I had to show my "or else"—or else. To say that Peggy grew self-confident is putting it mildly. She became a demon of terror with a bewildered teacher as military backing. Did this group of children learn to love each other? You should have seen the hate rattling around in those ten little eyeballs during the lesson. I felt like calling her Metal Mouth myself. Since then I have run into several teachers and parents who have experienced the same dilemma. Many children will run to the bishop, Mom and Dad, or teachers whenever they feel snubbed.

My favorite strategy, before learning about group dynamics, was to zero in on the popular child. I'd flatter him by making him class captain. I'd go out of my way to be an adult friend by interviewing him, consulting him, praising him. Then, when the relationship was ripe, I'd take him aside and give him the responsibility to "friendship" an outcast. Developing a friendship with a popular child, any child, is great. We need to do that. But changing a person's mind about a particular child does very little to change his general attitude. I essentially knelt before King Johnny and begged him to adopt poor Melanie into his kingdom. His leadership tactics are still the same. His peer power remains manipulative. Suppose he graciously decides to let Melanie be "in." Our Primary class is peaceful. But what about next year? In fact, there's about a fifty-fifty chance that Melanie gets a break only during Primary, when the teacher is looking. Meanwhile, Johnny still controls his friends, including the one he just added. And his serfs are still quaking before each other. I probably solidified his position even more by catering to his power. Parents do the same thing when, for example, they plead with an older brother to "take it easy" on Junior.

We could go on exploring the hundreds of ways in which problems can be created or multiplied by single-symptom doctoring, rushing from one side effect to another. But there is no need for any of us to get dragged into that kind of madhouse of childhood politics. There are ways to help everyone at the same time, because all people within the peer group have the same basic needs. They all need self-esteem and unconditional acceptance. They all need opportunities to contribute to the group and extend love toward others. We can help them meet these needs without singling out any particular individual. They can all learn together. With a few simple principles in the front of our minds, and a few simple strategies, we as adults can make a tremendous difference. Any adult can teach any group of children how to love one another.

2

You Can Teach Them to Love One Another

Most children associate with the same group of young-sters for many years. Parents understand this better than other adults; they know that brothers and sisters spend ten to twenty years living together in the same home. It's harder for a teacher to realize this fact. Every time I meet a class for the first time, it's easy to think, "Well, here's a new class." In reality, however, this group of youngsters may have known each other for five or six years already, progressing together from one teacher to the next. *I'm* the new kid in town. The older the children, the more experiences they have shared. Their relationships are continually changing, and it is important that I know how those relationships are progressing at the moment when I intrude upon their world.

First, we will discuss how good relationships are built. Then we will get to the business of evaluating what kind of help any given group of children need to experience deeper affection for one another.

The Love Ladder

Meaningful relationships are built over time. They progress step by step as people learn to trust each

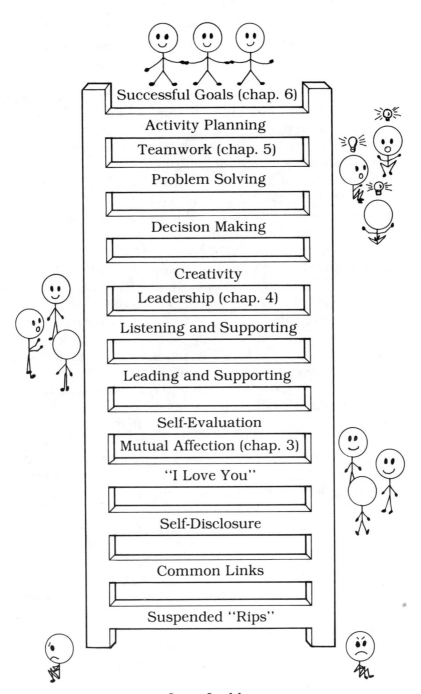

Successful Goals (chap. 6)

Activity Planning

Teamwork (chap. 5)

Problem Solving

Decision Making

Creativity

Leadership (chap. 4)

Listening and Supporting

Leading and Supporting

Self-Evaluation

Mutual Affection (chap. 3)

"I Love You"

Self-Disclosure

Common Links

Suspended "Rips"

Love Ladder

other and share successful experiences together. The accompanying figure summarizes the steps a group of people need to take in order to maximize their love for one another.

Assuming that a group of children are completely alienated toward one another, they would need to start at the bottom of the ladder and work up, step by step. Note that the ladder is divided into four major stages. The goal of the first stage, mutual affection, is to produce good feelings between them. Steps leading to those feelings create an atmosphere of safety and trust. When we bring our children through this stage, we establish a foundation of security that will enable them to venture into higher realms of cooperation and teamwork. They can acknowledge, without fear, the changes they need to make in their behavior. They can boldly try different ways to help each other succeed.

We begin by gagging "cuts" or "rip-downs." By suspending as much as possible quarrelling and verbal abuse, we essentially put away the guns that can blast away any positive experience. Then we can ease children into liking each other by helping them to find similarities between themselves. Once we establish common links, we can deepen their relationships with self-disclosure. By sharing each other's dreams, hopes, fears, opinions, talents, testimonies, and doubts, they gradually develop trust. Exchanging personal information fosters understanding and acceptance. When they feel comfortable talking about themselves, we can then introduce them to various ways of expressing approval and love for one another.

Most parents and teachers are striving for mutual affection as the ultimate goal. A group of children who are comfortable and happy together would appear to love each other, and this is true in a limited sense. But it is unfortunate that many are satisfied with this phase of development and thus fail to strive for higher levels of cooperation and understanding.

Children can be bonded together much more strongly if they can successfully achieve goals together. It is no accident that families like the Osmonds, the Kings, and the Von Trapps are woven tightly into strong units of love and loyalty. For the family "business" to succeed, every single member is important. Every person is needed. Everyone must learn to cooperate with everyone else. Success brings a feeling of joint accomplishment: "We did it together!" Each person can identify with the family and draw upon it for strength in times of personal crisis. The same is true with friends in a church class. If you can create this strong bonding between your children, they'll be invincible against the world. They have a cheering section to help them reach for their highest potential. They are much more likely to develop their testimonies, go on missions, marry in the temple, earn academic laurels, rise in their occupational fields. Most importantly, they find happiness and love in a dog-eat-dog world. Success breeds success. The more goals you can help your children reach together, the stronger they become. Their need to be needed, to have responsibility and respect, will be met in the family or among their friends.

Most of us have neither the time nor the resources to start a full-time family business. By providing a few key experiences, however, we can achieve the same results. Some years ago I went to a cousin's mission farewell in a ward I had once lived in. A group of young teenagers came up to me, apparently very excited. "Do you remember me?" one of the girls asked hopefully. I guessed, "Primary class?" She looked pleased. Then I remembered. Yes, it was a seven-year-old class of four girls and two boys. I remembered that this ward regularly lost young people as they entered Mutual. I looked at the teenagers and made a quick count. Four girls and two boys! Looking at them, though, I couldn't remember which girl was the smart alec, which boy was the sullen rebel, or which girl cowered under rejection. They all seemed like good friends. How did I feel? Besides feeling like an old lady, I was very surprised. This was one of my accidental successes that I had stumbled into before my formal education. Unwittingly I had done the right thing by helping these kids plan and put on a talent show just for each other. It was so simple, and yet they still remembered it. They still talked about it. It had made a difference.

One reason this success surprised me was that I had failed so many times with other children. In fact, when I tried the same talent-show routine on another seven-year-old class, it fell apart. So did a couple of the children, who ran home crying brokenheartedly because their peers laughed at them. One success for every ten failures is not a good track record. The next two stages on the Love Ladder prevent the failures, preparing children for achieving goals together successfully. Since I started using the system, it has never failed me.

We move up the ladder by encouraging children to evaluate their own behavior toward other people. Then we teach them alternate ways of leading and supporting one another. The leadership stage forces each child to evaluate himself and offers skill practice in the changes he wants to make. The bully decides to be a democratic leader. The silent member decides to contribute. The popular manipulator decides to listen to suggestions and delegate responsibility.

The teamwork stage throws everyone together into cooperative tasks. The tasks, however, are highly specialized and progress from simple to complex. First, we can teach children how to brainstorm. Neglecting to brainstorm properly is one of the biggest reasons for failures in committees. There are a few simple guidelines to brainstorming that enhance group creativity without stifling individuality. Once people are adept at whipping out ideas, they are ready

to learn how to narrow choices down to a single decision. Much destructive conflict can be avoided if
decisions are made systematically. The problem-
solving step combines previous skills and offers practice on fantasy problems.

In the final stage, you as an adult leader guide your
children through planning and implementing an activity. The activity is a teaching tool, a dress rehearsal for
the time when they are set loose on their own independent goals. If you follow the guidelines suggested in
chapter 6, your children will gain not only mutual
love, but a tremendous advantage in the world. Most
adults have difficulty working together in groups because they have never been taught how to do so. In a
society in which group cooperation is a daily fact of
life, anyone who can facilitate more productive teamwork will enjoy great personal success. Whatever their
occupation, your children will find satisfaction working with other people. Engineers need each other to
design complex technical products. Politicians need
each other to operate cities, school boards, and sen-
ates. Parents need each other to make needed changes
in their communities.

The important thing to remember about the Love
Ladder is that each step is a necessary prerequisite for
the step above it. This fact explains why my previous
experiments had mixed results. If my class members
had a serious problem with cutting each other down,
my attempts to get them to say "I love you" (three
steps up) always failed. It was too much to ask. They
just weren't prepared to make that giant leap. In fact,
the result could do more harm than good. ("I love her
because she has zits"; "I don't love him, I hate him.")
When I did something that worked, it was either pure
luck that it didn't backfire, or I just happened to be on
the right step of the ladder for that group of students.
Before doing anything else, you need to decide where
your children are on the Love Ladder today.

To begin with, an understanding of basic group

development phases can help explain why your children may be acting the way they are. After a brief review of these phases, a survey questionnaire will help you evaluate your children's relationships.

They're Going Through a Phase

We've all heard of child development, the phases of learning and emotions that we can expect from a child at different times in his life. We use this understanding to plan our adult-to-child strategy to maximize his abilities and happiness. Groups have life spans too. Understanding the group process can help us plan our strategies more intelligently.

Adults may go through all four of the following phases in a single hour because they have practiced the process so many times in the past. Children, however, may spend years in a single phase, groping through their first social experience. Parents should keep in mind that this process is going on at church and school. Their children will bring their successes and failures home to their brothers and sisters. Every family I worked with showed definite parallels between the way their children were getting along with their peers and how they acted at home.

Phase 1: Encounter. When people are thrown together for the first time they feel insecure. *How am I supposed to act?* they wonder. *Is this someone I'm supposed to like? What do these people think of me?* Every one of us has experienced this terrible feeling at one time or another. When I am thrust into a group of strangers, I feel as if I'm floundering in the ocean, trying to keep my head above water. If there's a floating object anywhere in sight I grab for it. That is what people do in these first few tense moments. They cling to the only stable object in sight: the formal leader—the host, boss, teacher, or parent, the one in charge.

Children meeting each other formally for the first time—at church or school—rely almost exclusively on the teacher for approval and acceptance. They also experience tremendous anxiety and will change their behavior radically from week to week, sometimes venting their insecurity with "bad" behavior. Angels one week are disruptive the next, and vice versa. This phase is the best possible time to begin group training. Their cooperation is high, their eagerness to learn is at a peak, and their social slate is blank. These children need lots of affection and tightly secured rules.

Phase 2: Testing. During this stage group members still look to the leader for guidance, but continually test that leader to determine acceptable behavior. More than anything else, individuals are testing to see how much other people are willing to mobilize against the "boss." They will try something "daring" and watch both peers and boss for reactions. "What happens if I don't answer this question?" "What happens if I poke fun at this other person?" "What happens if I lean back in my chair?"

For children in Primary, this period lasts until they are about six years old. At school, it goes through first grade into second grade. Again, the teacher has a great deal of influence over the way children will perceive themselves and each other. Concrete rules for behaving help diffuse much of the discomfort they experience, and proper guidance can prevent many of the problems that occur later on.

Phase 3: Norm setting. This is perhaps the most important phase. During this time, group members decide on values, unspoken rules of conduct, and forms of punishment and rewards for conforming to those rules. For example, a group may decide that jeans are the thing to wear, and that polyester slacks are definitely not. Anyone wearing polyester slacks is sentenced to unrelenting teasing, silent rejection, or some other form of pressure to conform. At this time social roles begin to form. People no longer shift between various kinds of behavior, but begin to act consistently as leader, joker, bully, dunce, follower, winner, or loser.

Children experience a rigidity in their relationships at about seven years old. Adults begin to lose their influence as peer leaders assert their power. During the norm-setting stage, anxiety reaches a peak and destructive behavior may climb during the war of roles and rules. Children become like butterflies struggling out of their cocoons, jousting among themselves for control, anxiously searching for their places in the group. Children at this phase have a monumental task before them, setting up the constitution of their first social group, and it often impedes other important learning activities such as reading, adding numbers, or preparing for baptism.

This is one of the most challenging times as far as discipline is concerned. It is tempting to rule with an iron hand, but it is important during this time for the adult to negotiate with the children to come up with mutually agreeable rules. A CTR teacher in our ward has a natural talent for this kind of compromise. "I want them to be reverent during opening exercises," she told me, "but they hate to do cute little stand-up-and-stretch exercises with the 'little kids' during song practice. So I said, 'Hey, you don't have to stand up if you don't want to. But I do expect you to show quiet respect for the chapel.' They agreed to this and do just fine." Children in this stage are still willing to work with adults and are usually flexible about rules, as long as they have things their way once in a while. During this time a teacher or parent can make a tremendous impact on the future of those children by participating in the formation of group rules.

Phase 4: Production. During this phase, group members settle into their respective roles and become comfortable with their rules. The group becomes "intact."

Adult power practically disappears as the children exercise independent group force. As time goes on, role behavior intensifies—passive children become

more passive, frustrated children become more disruptive, leader types become more assertive.

Attempts to change roles will probably be rejected.
Children have the most rigid caste systems in the
world. I remember a boy in a nine-year-old class who
always knew the answers. He was the "egghead" of
the group. At one of our class parties, this boy pulled a
silly prank on another boy. "What's with you all of a
sudden?" the others asked with some irritation. It
didn't matter that two other boys had just pulled a
similar trick. They were the "cut-ups" and were there-
fore expected to act like clowns. Their joke was greeted
with peals of laughter.

If the group is poorly formed, it will break up into
opposing cliques, each operating under its own set of
rules—boys vs. girls, cut-ups vs. eggheads, rich vs.
poor, older vs. younger. Very often the entire group is
torn by intense competition. This phase is really the
acid test for relationships. If the atmosphere is friendly
and comfortable, group members can easily be made
into a productive unit that can solve real problems in
council meetings, initiate and organize parties, and
plan and carry out service projects, class presentations, and even whole lessons. If not, frustration en-
sues whenever the group is given a task. Adults who
have experienced these frustrations throughout their
lives will complain about "committee elephants." One
or two people typically end up doing all the work,
others are never given a chance to contribute, still
others feel disgusted when long meetings produce no
results.

In a family of mixed ages, you are likely to find at
least two of the above behavior symptoms among your
children. The younger ones are probably more easy-
going than the older ones. Most of the time it is the
older children who have trouble going up the Love
Ladder. For example, most families with children over
seven years old have problems with them cutting each

other down verbally. Every family I've worked with
certainly did. If this is true in your family, don't feel
bad about it! It has nothing to do with family life; your
children are bringing home their anxieties and poor
coping habits from school. Remember that they are in
the middle of a terrible adjustment phase with their
friends at school and church. They are in the norm-
setting or even production phase in their relationships.
They pick up the war language and bring it home. If
you can help them find a haven of peace at home
where they don't need to prove themselves, you have
accomplished a great deal toward their happiness.

An Evaluation Survey

Where are your children on the Love Ladder? The
following survey will help you determine their status.
Refer to this questionnaire often as you progress
through this book.

Cuts. Think about and answer the following questions. Be careful not to insert yourself in the picture:
This is not an evaluation of your relationships with
your children. What is it like among *them?*

1. How often do they cut each other down?
    (Never / Sometimes / Often / Constantly)
2. How much time do you spend settling argu-
    ments when the family or class is involved to-
    gether in discussions, outings, and so on?
    (None / Sometimes / Often / Constantly)
3. Are there serious negative feelings between two
    or more of your children?
4. To what extent do cuts disturb family/class
    peace?
    (Very little / Quite a bit / A great deal)

Even if only two or three of your children are ripping
each other down, start at the bottom of the ladder
(chapter 3). It won't hurt your other children to go
along for the ride. In fact, they can help move the
family or class more rapidly up the ladder. Though all
strategies suggested in this book are group oriented

and avoid spotlighting any individuals, you should remember which children need the most work and start
everyone on that level. If your children have no serious
"ripping" problems, move on to the next set of questions.

Self-Disclosure:

1. Do your children tell each other about their
   daily activities and accomplishments?
   (Never / Sometimes / Often / Constantly)
2. Do your children talk about their feelings with
   each other—their fears, doubts, hopes, dreams?
   (Never / Sometimes / Often / Constantly)
3. How would you describe your children's attitude when you ask them to share talents with
   each other?
   (Uncooperative / Reluctant / Willing / Eager)

If your children never talk about their activities or feelings with each other, and dread performing in front of
one another, begin with lower-level activities on the
self-disclosure step (chapter 3). If they seem to do these
things occasionally or on a superficial basis, you can
start with higher-level activities on the same step. If
they feel completely comfortable sharing themselves
with each other, skip this step and move on to the next
set of questions.

"I Love You":

1. How often do you hear your children praising
   each other?
   (Never / Sometimes / Often / Constantly)
2. How often do your children show physical affection, such as a hug, kiss, pat on the back?
   (Never / Sometimes / Often / Constantly)
3. Do your children feel comfortable saying "I love
   you" to each other?
   (Can't say it / Can say it with prompting / Say it
   easily and often)

If your children are unable to praise each other, show
physical affection, or say "I love you," begin with
lower-level activities on the "I love you" step (chapter

3). If they can do all of the above things occasionally or with prompting on your part, you can start them on higher-level experiences. If they have no problems doing the above, they already enjoy mutual affection. Move on to the next set of questions.

Leadership Skills:

1. Do one or two children make all the decisions among your group?
2. How does the "leader" influence his/her peers or siblings?
   (Bullying / Charming / Involving everyone)
3. How many of the other children seem confident about expressing their own opinions?
4. Do they take turns being in charge?
   (Never / Rarely / Sometimes / Constantly)

Your children practice good leadership skills if they consistently share responsibilities. Those of approximately the same age should be equally involved in contributing suggestions and making plans. All of your children should feel confident enough to express their own opinions and take turns leading the others. If they are not able to exercise this kind of leadership, begin on the self-evaluation step (chapter 4). If they already act this way, move on to the next set of questions.

Listening Skills:

1. How well do they listen to each other? Are they talking without responding to what another child has just said?
   (Poor / Fair / Good / Excellent)
2. When one child is speaking, do the others ask relevant questions about his/her topic?
   (Rarely / Sometimes / Most of the time / Always)
3. How often do misunderstandings occur because one child did not correctly hear what another child said?
   (Never / Sometimes / Constantly)

Your children should rank an "excellent" on the first question. They should always respond appropriately to what someone else has just said. Sometimes people are so busy thinking about what they want to say that they don't hear what is being said at the moment. The clearest sign that this is going on is in their responses. Example: Child A, "I got an A in English!" Child B, "Hey, let's go to the park!" Child B ignored what Child A was saying. If misunderstandings occur frequently because your children simply didn't hear each other correctly, they need practice in listening skills. Start them on the self-evaluation step, then move to listening skills (chapter 4). If your children pass on this category, they don't need individual behavior change. They are prepared to learn teamwork skills. Move on to the next set of questions.

Creativity. Think about your children's responses to open-ended questions during family or class discussions, such as: "What would you do in this situation?" "What are ways we can show reverence?"

1. Are there long periods of silence after you ask an open-ended question?
   (Never / Sometimes / Always)
2. How many of your children tell their ideas without prompting?
3. When asked to brainstorm, how many ideas does each child generate compared to the other children? (List each child and decide whether his typical input of ideas is low, average, or high compared to the others.)
4. Do they tend to follow the same line of thought?
5. Do they look to you for the "right" answer?
6. Do they frequently interrupt the flow of ideas to judge specific suggestions as they come along?

When brainstorming for ideas, your children should be able to jump right in and whip the thoughts out rapidly. Ideas should come just about equally from everyone and range far and wide in variety and direction. For example, when you ask, "What can we do to show reverence?" you should hear not only ways to prepare for prayer (one line of thought), but ways of thinking and acting in church, family, school, or alone. They should be able to brainstorm without pausing to throw out or favor specific ideas. If they need practice in brainstorming, start on the creativity step (chapter 5).

Decision Making/Problem Solving

1. When you give your children a decision to make together, do they explore many different possibilities first?
   (Rarely / Sometimes / Always)
2. Do they have a tendency to "rubber stamp" one child's ideas?
3. Can they reach a decision or pick a final solution without your help?
   (Rarely / Sometimes / Always)

When making group decisions, your children should automatically brainstorm first, then systematically narrow their choices down. There should be some healthy conflict (not ripping each other down, but legitimate disagreements and aggressive negotiating about solutions). If they reach decisions too quickly and quietly, they are probably "rubber stamping" one youngster's decisions. They should be able to work out their problems without running to you for help. If you think they could use some improvement in this area, start on the decision-making step (chapter 5).

Reaching Successful Goals. Evaluate the children's ability to plan, organize, and successfully complete group assignments together. Examples of such assignments would be family outings, class parties, family home evenings, service projects, a Primary activity day, a food storage plan, a Scout trip, or a family garden. These should be carried out without your leadership.

1. Do they brainstorm many different possibilities?

2. Do they all participate equally in making decisions?
3. Do they all share responsibilities equally?
4. Do they seem satisfied with their work?
5. Rate the success of most of their independently planned goals.
   (Poor / Fair / Good / Excellent)

The teamwork stage involves mostly brainwork. The final stage on the Love Ladder is the acid test. What can they *do* together, "for real"? Often a group of children who can go through make-believe problems just fine will fall apart when it comes to the real thing. Chapter 6 will help you guide your children through their first formal experience together, using the activity as a teaching model for their meeting future challenges alone.

How to Structure Each Learning Experience

The strategies in this book can be used with as few as two children or as many as fifteen. But for maximum success, child groups should have between five and ten members. Appropriate groups for these exercises are Primary classes, families with at least three children between the ages of three and twelve, and formal play groups (parent-run preschools, for example). If you have teenagers in the family, explain to them in private what you are trying to do for the younger children and enlist their help and cooperation. Teenagers don't like "kid games" and will often thwart your efforts if you try to include them with the younger ones. Approaching them before any training sessions will put them on your side; as long as you recognize them as separate, they'll be amazingly cooperative.

Most of the activities in this book have variations suggested for younger or older children. If you have a mixed-age group, choose older versions and devise ways for the older children to help the younger ones participate. You need to structure your games around the abilities and interests of your older children because they are the most inhibited. They need the most help. A quick review of the group phases explained earlier in this chapter helps show why. Your little ones are actually more advanced in social skills. They express love more spontaneously. You'll find they can actually help the others up the Love Ladder.

Each activity suggested in this book is a modified version of an adult training session. The purpose of the games is to provide good experiences between children, every bit as valuable as "real" experiences in everyday interaction. These experiences, however, have a specific purpose: to teach social skills in a palatable way. There is no reason why you should have to rigidly structure the games exactly the way they are presented here. If a suggestion can be modified in its application from adult to child, it can easily be modified to fit your precise situation. Take the suggestions provided and build your own creative store of fun and joy. Your greatest resource for ideas is your own imagination!

Every session should have three basic steps, each of which is important for your children. First, explain the goal you are trying to achieve with the activity. This can take anywhere from thirty seconds to fifteen minutes, depending on how much you want to elaborate. Try not to make an hour-long lecture out of it. It can be as simple as saying, "Tonight we're going to explore things we have in common with each other. By doing this we should feel more united as a family (class)."

By plainly expressing goals before you begin, you achieve two results. For one thing, explaining helps develop trust and respect between you and your children. Today's youth are far more sophisticated than those of twenty or even ten years ago. Do you like it when somebody tries to trick you into doing something? Do you like to be manipulated? Neither do your children. I have learned that children will act as responsibly as I treat them. If they feel I don't trust them, they'll do anything in their power to thwart my sneaky plan. Wouldn't you?

One particularly rowdy six-year-old once came up to me and said, "I like you. You know why?" Startled, I replied, "No, I haven't the faintest idea." Then he puffed out his proud little chest and said, "First, because you laugh a lot. Second, because you don't treat me like a stupid kid." That's today's rascal. Since the children know you're up to something, you might as well tell them what it is. Youngsters respond to honesty. They will try to make your goal succeed.

Stating the goal also helps your children to glean from their "experience" what you want them to learn. It focuses their attention on the right lesson. I've heard the story of Chicken Little many times in various settings, each with an entirely different message. If the speaker didn't bother to explain what his message was, chances are I wouldn't get the lesson Chicken Little was supposed to teach me that day. Every story, parable, visual aid, or activity can illustrate hundreds of different lessons. If I don't pinpoint the exact goal of an activity, the children will probably miss the point, or fail to learn it as thoroughly as I want them to.

The second step of your session is to run the activity. Activities are suggested in this book for each step on the Love Ladder.

Third, and most important, process the experience. This involves asking a series of discussion questions to help the children generalize what they learned to their relationships. Processing helps to assure internalization and lasting effect. Be sure to plan for enough processing time at the end of the session. Though questions are suggested with exercises in this book, you may want to create your own to fit your particular group. When making up questions, use the following guidelines:

1. Get your children to talk about what happened
   during the "game" and how they felt while they
   were playing it.
2. Then get them to discuss what they learned
   from the experience. What insights did they
   receive?
3. Finally, try to get them to apply what they
   learned to everyday living. How can they use
   their new insights to improve their relationships?

How much should adults become involved during
the exercise? Younger children need more supervision
than older ones, but stay as unobtrusive as possible.
Try to stay out while the children learn and practice
emerging skills among themselves. Let them make
mistakes. Enforce the rules which have been clearly
stated in the beginning, but resist the temptation to
police every move. The goal, after all, is to help them
learn how to relate to one another without adult inter-
ference. If things don't go the way you want them to,
take advantage of whatever happens by getting your
children to talk and analyze it during processing time.

A common problem among the families I have
worked with is undue anxiety over "cheating." We
have a tendency to believe that if the children are
having fun they're not learning. Just remember that
the loopholes your children find in the game rules
were meant to be found; the loopholes guide them into
the right behavior. The biggest concern of adults
seems to be sincerity. If the behavior isn't "sincere,"
adults seem to feel that the children are getting away
with some trickery, and they want to throw the activity out: "That doesn't count—you're cheating!"

We need to recall how we ourselves develop desirable habits. I remember how I learned to pray. First I
said a bunch of words in the arms of my mother. She
seemed pleased, so I practiced being "reverent" and
making my prayers "right." As I grew older, prayer
became a daily habit, though rarely meaningful. As

problems came along, I tried real communication with our Father and discovered that prayer works. So prayer became, over the years, a truly valuable tool for personal security and happiness. Suppose my mother had slapped my little hands and said, "You're not being sincere! It doesn't count because you're cheating!" I would have been crushed. I would have been afraid to try again. If I had never prayed before, how could I know what a sincere prayer was?

Any skill is awkward at first. It appears stilted and "plastic." In our impatience to get our children to be genuine we can kill the very trait we want to develop. Encourage your children whenever they try, no matter how "fake" it looks. After enough "faking," they'll eventually become truly sincere.

One last suggestion: Enjoy it! These games are fun! Children love them. They're lumps of sugar that happen to carry important lessons in them. Approach these activities with a sense of humor and excitement —and relax.

3

Mutual Affection:

"I Like Being with You"

"They're just teasing each other."

But the cutting words that fly through the air are just as dangerous to the spirit as poison darts would be to the body. Why do children cut each other down? It is a primitive way to establish pecking orders and social rules. The process is very similar to behavior in a chicken coop. Tiny chicks start off almost immediately to peck at each other. Eventually one chicken emerges at the top of the heap, and gets to peck at all the other chickens. Number Two chicken can peck any other chicken except Number One. The system works all the way to the bottom to the poor chicken who gets pecked by a dozen other birds, but never pecks back. The order is confirmed every day. Number One makes it a point to peck everybody else. Number Two pecks everyone below him. The bottom chicken endures a life of constant misery.

People do similar things to each other—often deciding social roles and rules with the same barbarity. It is a gladiator game to see who can outrip the others for a higher social position. Once the superior position is won, it is kept with never-ending duels. This is a common problem in the adult business world. A supervisor often feels compelled to verbally abuse his subordinates in order to advertise his authority. Sometimes an entire organization is a classic chicken coop, its pecked employees either leaving or performing poorly.

One of the reasons I hate rip-downs so much is because they effectively block progress. If you have a serious problem with cuts in your family or class, and you ignore it, I guarantee complete failure with any other suggestion in this book. This unpleasant problem must have first priority.

Rips are statements that attack other children: "You're dumb"; "I hate you"; "Nerd-face." Refer to the survey section in chapter 2; answer the questions under "cuts" and decide if you will need to concentrate on reducing verbal abuse. If the problem occurs sporadically, the other sections in this chapter offer positive ways to displace much of the negative talk that may appear once in a while. This section is for chronic problems. Its goal is to gag rip-downs, not necessarily to produce good feelings between the children. Good feelings come with upbeat experiences.

Young children rarely have serious problems with rip-downs. I had only one class under five years old that needed help in this area, and the problem was cleared up in two weeks. I've met very few other teachers or parents who complained about such behavior. Sometimes families will have sharp-witted little ones who imitate or fight back older siblings. If you have a young group (between three and five years old) with a problem with cuts, you can easily guide them away. Your influence is so powerful that you can control spitfires by simply making a rule: We never say things that hurt. At the end of each class or family dinner time, reward each individual child who kept the rule with praise, a hug, a star—whatever suits your style. Do not scold or give attention to the child who failed. Simply leave him out of the praise. The problems should peter out within three weeks for teachers, three days for parents. I like this approach because I don't have to focus negative attention on anyone. (Attention of any kind can actually encourage a repeat performance.) Small children will quickly shed behaviors that block them from the warmth they hunger for, especially when they see others basking in your approval.

Constant negative verbal exchanges are not uncommon, however, among older children. Even when they seem to be only ribbing each other, they are really setting norms, punishing "offenders" and establishing social positions. We already know that this easy way out for solving problems is not healthy for anyone.

Try a suspended rule first: We don't rip each other during class / family home evening. One parent told me she gets her family to suspend rips during dinner and family discussions. "Even though they continue to cut each other at other times, at least we can have meaningful times together." This kind of rule needs to be in place during any activity from this book, and generally it works. There are groups, however, who can't even handle a cease-fire for one hour. I had two classes like that; it's not unusual for families to get overwhelmed by the problem as well.

A warring group nearly always has a few key weaknesses. You can take advantage of those weaknesses to strengthen your children. Such a group, for example, is nearly always competitive to the extreme. They are obsessed with beating each other. They can't stand to lose. (I once had a class so competitive that when I asked, "What do you like to do on Saturday?" they fought over who gave the best answer.) Another weakness, ironically, is their great dependence on each other for acceptance. This makes it easy for you to set up the structure, then step aside and let them gag each other. Use their competitive spirit by giving them a joint goal. They compete against time. The rules of the game can hinge on what they say to each other. I used the following strategy for an eight-year-old class of five boys and one girl. Each member was incredibly sharp-witted, quick to rip anyone to shreds who ventured a contribution to the lesson. Bad feelings and hopeless lessons nearly drove me bananas. In two months, however, the atmosphere took a 180-degree turn, thanks to the Goal Chart that follows.

The Goal Chart can work for families, too, but I've discovered that families need to set aside a certain amount of time each day when the game is "on." Parents who tried the chart on a twenty-four-hour-a-day basis were hard-pressed to concentrate all day on earned points and keep their children interested in the chart for two long months. One or two hours a day, preferably in a consistent time frame, should make it easier on the whole family. The Goal Chart should be in operation as you introduce your children to other activities in the book. You want them to climb as many steps up the Love Ladder as they can before their goal is reached. The farther along they are on the ladder, the less likely they are to revert back to chronic ripping.

Goal Chart

I made a poster chart (see accompanying illustration) that promised a camping trip at the end of two months *if* the children earned 300 points by the deadline. When deciding on a reward, pick something the group can get excited about. One parent I know played it safe and said, "If you make the goal we'll use fifty dollars to do anything you want to do as a family." The children earn points when they say kind things to each other. They lose points every time you hear a rip-down. For this to work, it is important for you to state the rules clearly and completely. The following is a summary of my particular point system. When making up your own point system, make sure that rip-downs are devastating losses. Note how my eight-year-olds had to work on five upbeat statements to recover from a single cut.

Upbeat (+1). Comments that support someone else's contribution to the class or family. For example: "I agree," "You have a good point there," "Thank you," "Please," "That's a great idea," "I like that," "I think you're right," "You're welcome." There has to be a legitimate reason for saying something upbeat. Repeats don't count (in other words, they can't stand in front of you and say "Please, please, please, please, please" and get five points). Sarcasm counts as a rip-down.

Rip-down (–5). Anything that rips down another person or his ideas. This includes the teacher and the lesson. *It's all right to disagree with someone as long as it isn't a personal attack.* Instead of saying, "That's a dumb thing to say," say, "I disagree, because . . ."

Build-up (+5). At the beginning of every class or family gathering (dinner time worked best for the families I worked with), each person gets a chance to earn five points with a build-up. This means the class/family can earn twenty to twenty-five points immediately if they are prepared. Each person is to find something he admires about another person in the group and to express it. General comments don't count. Statements that aren't true don't count. A person cannot build up the same person twice until he has done everyone in the group. (This rule assures that no one is consistently left out.)

> Bad example: He's good at sports (too general).
> Good example: He's great to have on a baseball team. I saw him hit a home run last week during an important game.

I suggest that you demonstrate what good build-ups are by expressing something positive about each of your children, instead of using my examples above. Present a bad example and a good example for each child. Not only will you be setting an example for

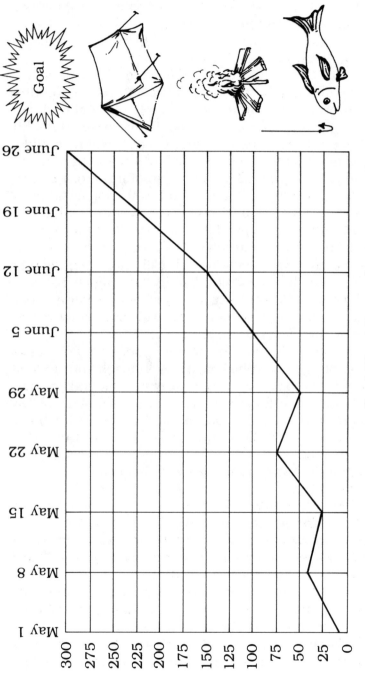

Goal Chart Example

them, but they will love hearing what you like about them. Be helpful the first few times. If the compliment is too general, patiently help them expand it and praise them liberally for trying.

Fair Judge (+ 10). This category is optional. It seems to work better during a structured lesson time, so if you do use it in the family I suggest you try it only during family home evening. Every week one child will be a judge, the one who decides when to add or subtract points. You, as the teacher or parent, will decide if the judge did a good job of monitoring. If the judge is too easy or too hard, all positive points earned that day will be wiped out, while negative points will count. If he does a good job, he earns ten points for the goal. His whole attention should be focused on upbeats and rip-downs. I like to have the children be judges because they learn a great deal by judging each other's statements. By deciding for themselves, over and over again, a good comment from a bad, they become sensitive to their own comments.

If you don't want to appoint a judge, you can quietly mark points on the board as you teach your lessons, careful not to pause or make any judgmental gestures. If dinner time is part of your cease-fire, Mom or Dad will have to eat cold potatoes and gravy for a while to record points. Be firm and consistent about points.

Sore Loser (– 10). The group automatically loses ten points if anyone argues with his teacher or parent over points.

It is important that your children understand the rules of the game thoroughly before you begin. It is also important that you remain friendly and impassive. Just say to yourself over and over again, "This is something they have to do on their own." Let them know that you care, that you're cheering for them, but that you aren't doing the work or changing the rules. The youngsters will pick up on your attitude. It will give them a greater sense of urgency. Resist the temptation to yell or scream the first couple of weeks.

You're not failing at all! Groups who are making radical changes in their constitution nearly always go through a period of testing. They may actually increase their ripping just to see what you do about it. If your children are normal, they will go in the hole. They may lose as many as fifty points before climbing up. Relax! As you calmly mark off the points and remain supportive, they'll eventually come around. By the way, this period of adjustment is the reason why you want to give them two to three months to reach their goal.

Use that three-month period to help your children go as high as they can on the Love Ladder. Many of the inherent reasons for ripping will be erased as they find their needs met in other ways. The higher they are on the ladder when the goal is reached, the less likely they are to revert back to cutting behavior. In any case, the goal chart experience will help them to suspend cuts for considerable periods of time while you help them mend their relationships.

When they have achieved their goal, discuss how the cease-fire has affected your family or class. Here are a few suggestions for lead questions: How did you feel while you were working on this goal? Have you noticed any improvements in our class / family? How are things better? Why do words make a difference in our feelings for one another?

LINKS: WHAT DO WE HAVE IN COMMON?

Friendships begin with similarities. People need to find something they have in common on which to build a new relationship. Anything you can do to help your children find links between each other will be an excellent way to ease them into love. Discovering common ground is a good beginning for groups with bad feelings because you aren't pushing them into "mushy stuff." It is the safest tactic for self-conscious youngsters.

Children who already like each other enjoy these kinds of exercises, too. In fact, I've noticed that the more they like each other to begin with, the more delight they take in linking games. And you will be surprised how much closer the children come to each other, even though they seemed to be good friends already. These kinds of activities are good supplements for lessons touching on our relationships with each other or God. For example, when I taught a CTR A lesson titled "I Am a Child of God," I followed a linking game with a discussion on how people in a family are the same in many ways. ("How are you and your brothers and sisters alike in your family?") Then I pointed out that even though we are all different from each other, we are also similar in many ways because we are all brothers and sisters in God's family. Linking games can be divided into three categories: brainstorm races, common experiences, and matching.

Brainstorm Races

These are most appropriate for mixed-age groups such as families, or for older classes. If you have enough children (six to fifteen) you can divide them into two or three groups to compete against each other. If not, they can race against time. Both methods create a lot of adrenalin and common links.

Family Fortune is a big hit with families. Tell them to make believe they have a common ancestor who finally died at the age of 150. He was a millionaire, but very odd. He wanted to leave his whole fortune to a group of his descendants, but he wanted to make sure they were really related to each other. He decided to give his million dollars to the group that could find the most things in common with each other. He figured that if people are part of the same family they have more similarities.

If you have only one group, tell them they have five minutes to dig up as many things as they can that they share in common. The more they come up with, the more fortune they win. The rest will go to a business partner in Puerto Rico. Suggested payoff: 5 items = $100, 10 items = $500, 20 items = $100,000, 30 items = $500,000, 50 items = $1,000,000. You can make the game even more fun by passing out play money as they come up with ideas, then counting the winnings at the end. Give them two points for every item that the entire group shares in common and one point for any item that two or more members share.

Family Fortune can easily be converted into other themes. The children could qualify for a special assignment together by finding similarities between themselves (to prove they can get along). The special assignment could be the first mission call to Russia, or a scouting expedition for a pioneer train. Suggested discussion questions: What do you think we were supposed to learn from this game? Were you surprised that you had so much in common? Given all the time in the world, how many things could you find that you have in common with each other? Do you feel better about each other after doing this? Why? How does this suggest a way for us to like someone we dislike or don't know?

Common Experiences

My favorite linking strategy is to create common experiences. You don't have to form a baseball team or take the group on a mission to provide a common experience.

For small children it can be as simple as drawing a picture. Next time you have "coloring time," make it a social time, too. Instead of giving each person a sheet of paper and a bucket of crayons, give a large sheet of paper to every two children. Tell them to draw a picture together. Each person must draw his partner as part of the picture. Don't make the same mistake I made once: While training a group of first-grade students, I forgot to give a very important piece of instruction. Imagine my cold shock to see them draw thick lines down the middle of their papers and blissfully color their own individual pictures! Be sure to tell your children that they are to draw one big picture together. They must not divide the paper in half. When they have finished, bring each pair of children to the front to explain their picture to everyone else. You can specify a theme for their pictures. They can meet Jesus together, play with pets together, ride a fire engine together, and so on. Suggested lead questions: Was it easy or hard to draw on the same picture? Why? Was it fun to see somebody draw a picture of you? Do you like the people in your picture? Why? Do you like the person you drew? Why?

Hypothetical situations are great for older children and mixed ages. Situations can be invented to suit any lesson, any group personality. Use your creative juices to provide many common experiences for your children. Divide them into pairs and have them solve a common problem together, then relate their "plot" to the others. They could be elves trying to outwit a dragon who sits on a pot of gold, archaeologists caught by a tribe of cannibals. If your youngsters are into "realism," place them in the middle of a compromising situation at school or at a friend's house.

Matching Games

Matching games are social puzzles. You challenge the children to match their individual characteristics with those of the others. These activities are most appropriate for larger groups. Children three to six years old love the Stand Up and Clap game. Each week I bring a child to the front and ask a few questions, such as "Who has brown hair like Mary's? Stand up!" "Who has black shoes like Aaron's? Clap your hands!" Little children love to move their bodies, to clap, stomp, wiggle, dance. Try to put these movements into any activity you plan.

For older children you can use a strategy often used by adult trainers to break the ice. Pass out game

---

Game Card
(Example for Younger Children)

_____
Name

1. Favorite Colors _____

_____

2. School _____

_____

3. Favorite TV Shows _____

_____

---

cards similar to the accompanying illustrations. The first, above, is a card for children with limited writing ability, ages seven to eight. The second, on the following page, is more like an adult card. Design a card that suits your group.

Give your children time to fill out the top of each category for themselves. Then have them circulate among the group to search for others who share the same answer. They are to write the name of anyone who "connects" under each category. Then spotlight each person and challenge the others to guess how he filled out his card. When you've finished, try the following discussion questions: What surprised you the most about what you learned about each other? How did you feel when you found something you had

Game Card
(Example for Older Children)

Name _____

School	Favorite Subjects	Favorite TV Programs	After-School Activities

in common with another person? Did you want to talk about it? Sometimes we feel uncomfortable around people we don't know very well. Sometimes we even dislike them. What can we do to help us like those people?

Now that your children have sharpened their awareness of each other through linking, they are ready to venture into a deeper relationship. They are prepared to go one step further by sharing themselves with each other.

SELF-DISCLOSURE

There is a wide range of risks involved in exchanging personal information, anywhere from telling our favorite color to expressing our deepest fears. The farther we venture into feelings, the more meaningful and trusting our relationships become when we find acceptance. Most children long to share their feelings and will discover a peace and joyful freedom when they feel safe enough to be "real." How much risk should you ask your children to take? Once again, refer to your questionnaire. Children who have difficulty sharing themselves with each other need to start with nonthreatening situations, such as To Tell the Truth and Comic Strip. Gradually build them up to more probing exercises. Some games in this section are progressive (for example, Puppet and Me and Celebrity Interview), meaning they start with nonpersonal information, then move into more and more personal disclosures. These kinds of self-disclosure games are my favorites because they assure a good experience while helping me pinpoint exactly where my children are. These are great if you're not sure how much your children can handle. Stop the exercise when children begin to fidget nervously or become agitated.

In addition to the games suggested here, you can deepen self-disclosure by spotlighting individuals, encouraging the children to share "show-and-tell" items, exchanging favorite quotations, and having them bear their testimonies.

Puppet and Me

This is by far the most popular self-disclosure game among the small children (ages three to six years) I've taught. Little ones have fluid imaginations, easily transporting themselves into lovable objects—a teddy bear, a doll, a puppet. Let your children create puppets with paper sacks, crayons, glue, cloth, anything you have on hand. Then seat them in a close semicircle around you. Explain to them that you will ask each of their puppets a few questions and that you will see who can remember everything the puppet says. Bring one child at a time to your side. Placing your arms around the child, talk directly to the puppet and ask questions such as the following (after you have asked one or two questions you can keep the other children's attention by quizzing them on the answers):

1. What is your name? (the child will make one up on the spot)
2. What is your favorite color?
3. What do you love to eat?
4. What is the scariest thing in the world?
5. What do you want more than anything else in the world?

Ask the other children: "Who likes_____ name of puppet)? Good! I like him too." Feature every child.

Processing questions: Did you know before how many different kinds of puppets there are? Each of your puppets is special and different, isn't it? Even though they are all different, we like all of them. Why? Are people like puppets? How? People are different, too. Can we like someone even though we are different? Why? Did you like it when the puppets told us their secrets? Do you have a friend you like to tell secrets to? We just told each other a lot of secrets. Does that mean we are all friends?

Older children can think of a person they want to be (such as an astronaut, cowboy, ballerina, scientist, or TV character) and imagine they are answering your questions as that character. Or they can pretend to be their favorite Bible or Book of Mormon personality. Be sure to upgrade the questions to suit their age and interests.

Sharing Me

This is another exercise for small children. Don't be surprised if this experience proves difficult for one or two of your little ones, who may not want to part with their possessions for even a few minutes. It should be handled with gentleness and kindness on your part. Don't push anyone into this activity. I've found that most children will rise to the occasion and grow from it. The feelings are often so positive that a reluctant youngster will eventually ask to participate.

Have each child bring his most prized possession and explain to everyone else why it is important to him. Lead a brief discussion on how we treat other people's things: Would you ever throw your precious thing on the floor, step on it, or smear it with mud? Why? How do you treat your object that you've just shown? Everybody feels the same way about his things. If someone gave you something special, how would you treat it?

Explain that they will now practice what they said. Have each child place his object on a table. (If a child refuses to give his object over, don't press him.) Have them sit down, then bring one child up at a time and have him give his object to somebody else. Explain that this person will keep the object only until the lesson is over, that he is to take good care of it so that it will be just as good as it is now. After your regular lesson, have the children retrieve their objects.

Discussion questions may include: Was it hard to let somebody else hold your precious thing? Why? Is your thing just as beautiful and safe as it was before? Whoever took care of it for you must be a very good friend to treat it so nicely. How do you feel about him? Would you let him take care of it again someday? Why? Sometimes we want to make friends with somebody. If we have something, what can we do with it to make friends? If somebody shares something with us, how do we take care of it so we can stay friends?

For children ages seven to nine, have them keep the object for a week. Be sure to provide packing materials (boxes, newspaper) for transportation. This only works with responsible youngsters.

For children ages ten to eleven, have each child write down a scripture verse that means the most to him, and a one- or two-page letter explaining how this verse has helped him in his life. Have him place the letter in an envelope and write his name on the front. Randomly pass the envelopes to different people. (If a child does not want to give his envelope away, don't insist on it.) Assign them the task of reading the papers you gave them once a day. Tell them they will each be writing a reply letter the following week. Tell them to think about what they will write, with the following guidelines in mind:

1. Why you feel the verse was a good choice.
2. Some thoughts that came from reading the letter.
3. How reading this letter has helped you this week.

The following week, allow them time to write their reply letters (spread them out by themselves), then place the replies in the envelopes and return them to the original owners.

Advertising Me

This is a good activity for seven- to eleven-year-olds. Have each child make an advertising brochure about himself and explain it to everyone else. Brochures can be made by stapling construction paper pages together and gluing magazine cutouts or objects into the "brochure." Processing questions for this activity might include: Did you find out something you didn't know before? What? Do you like someone in this room better than you did before we made our advertising brochures? Why? The more we know about other people, the more we understand and like them. How does this suggest a way to develop good feelings about people we don't know or dislike?

A variation to this theme is to have each child choose his favorite Bible character or scripture passage and explain why it means so much to him.

For younger children, give each child a large sheet of newsprint. Let them choose among precut magazine or coloring book pictures to paste a representation of their bedroom. Many cutouts of the following are suggested: beds, cribs, bookshelves, toy chests, windows, toys, doors, closets, and so on. Have each of the children explain his bedroom to the others.

Comic Strip

This game works well for eight- to eleven-year-olds. Each person draws a comic strip about an experience he had that no one else knows about. Provide them with newsprint, colored markers, and some kind of barrier to hide their drawings from each other. Collect the comic strips and shuffle them. Randomly stick them on the wall and label each one with a letter or number. Then pass out match-up sheets like the following:

_____ Skylar

_____ Randy

_____ Julie

_____ Terry

Have them match comic strips with names on their paper. After they've had a chance to guess, reveal the artist of each strip and encourage the artist to elaborate on the story. Discussion questions would be like those in the activity Advertising Me.

You can match this exercise with a case study from a Primary or home evening manual. For example, the Merrie Miss A manual has a lesson on the strength of mothers and daughters in the home. You may want to have the girls draw comic strips about how they might spend a future typical day as mothers.

For three- to four-year-olds, have them bring a picture of themselves doing something (family outing, birthday party, beach, and so on). Place the photographs randomly on the board. Point to one picture and have the group guess whose picture it is. Help each child explain what is happening in his picture.

Celebrity Interview

Because this exercise requires fairly good reading and writing skills, it is more appropriate for older children. Pair up the children. Give one child from each pair a hat, reporter's badge (can be made out of construction paper), note pad, and pencil. Tell the children to pretend that those with hats and badges are newspaper reporters. The others are to be themselves, but to pretend that they have suddenly become famous. It is the reporter's job to interview his celebrity and get as much information as he can. He is to be understanding and try to make his celebrity feel good about talking about himself. A good reporter listens carefully and takes notes. Give each reporter a sheet with the following questions and three to five minutes for his interview (the interviews should be conducted simultaneously in various parts of the room):

1. What is your full name?
2. How many people are in your family?
3. What is your favorite color?

4. What do you like to eat? What do you hate to eat?
5. If you had $100, what would you spend it on?
6. What makes you happy?
7. What kinds of things do you love?
8. What scares you the most?
9. What is the saddest thing that ever happened to you?
10. If you could have any wish come true, what would you wish for?

If your children become deeply involved in their conversations, let them go past the time limit. This is something you want to encourage! Then have the partners reverse roles. After everyone has been interviewed, ask the following processing questions: Think about how you felt as a celebrity. Did any of the questions make you feel uneasy? Which ones? Why do you suppose some questions are easier to answer than others? Why is it frightening to talk about deeply personal feelings? How did you feel when your reporter seemed to understand what you were saying? Would you feel good about having him for a friend? There's a very important thing about friendship that we were supposed to learn from these interviews. What is it?

Variation: Instead of interviewing celebrities, the children could interview each other as Mormons. Questions can deal with religion, testimony, or topics from the manual. Example:

1. What day in the week do you have church?
2. You seem very healthy. Has your religion helped you in this respect?
3. Are you going to be married in one of those temples? Why?
4. What do you love most about being a Mormon?
5. Why do you believe in God?
6. What is your greatest hope in life, and how will your religion fulfill that hope?

You may want to have the interviews conducted in front of the whole group, especially if you have fewer than six people involved. Celebrity Interview can be played several times by simply assigning different pairs with new questions.

Feelings Time Line

This is an abstract exercise best done by eight- to eleven-year-olds. Give each youngster a sheet of news-print and colored markers. Have everyone draw a time line of their feelings from the past week. You may want to show them an example by displaying your own time line (see accompanying illustration).

Have each person explain his time line, then ask your children the following processing questions: What kinds of feelings were harder to share than others? Why? How did you feel when you saw other time lines with similar emotions? What does this say about people we know and their feelings? Does this make you more comfortable about talking out your feelings with friends? Why?

For younger children, have them pick a color of crayon that shows the way they feel right now. Have them draw their feelings on a sheet of paper. Then let each child explain his drawing and color. Or if you wanted to tie this activity in with a home evening or Primary lesson, you could ask the children to draw and color their feelings for Jesus or President Kimball —or whatever fits the lesson.

Miniversity

This gives older children a chance to teach each other their skills, a deeper form of sharing. Pass out index cards and pencils. Tell the children to write their names and three things they are good at doing (such as pitching a ball, making hair ribbons, saving money). Collect the cards. Next, create a Miniversity sign-up sheet by writing down on a poster or black-board, in random order, all items from all cards. Do not indicate who the "teachers" are for any category. Let your children sign up for three classes they want to

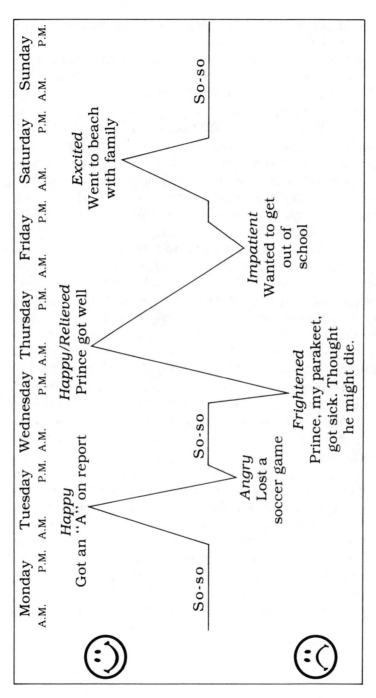

Time Line Example

take at the Miniversity. This is all you do during the first session.

Assign a "teacher" to each child. This can be done outside of class or family home evening. Warn the teachers ahead of time to give them a chance to prepare their lessons. Next time you meet as a group, give each pair of children sufficient time for one child to teach the other his subject. The following week, or after a break, reverse roles and assign new teachers to different students. All children who were students the first time should be teachers the second. If they maintain enthusiasm for Miniversity, you can continue the activity indefinitely or encourage them to continue teaching each other on their own time.

Processing questions: What did you learn at Miniversity that you didn't know before? Did you ever realize before how much you can teach each other? Why do you suppose people don't tell each other what they can do? Why are people afraid to ask somebody else to teach something they want to learn? What do you think about that? Are you going to be that way? Next time you want to learn something that one of your friends seems good at, what are you going to do? Next time you see one of your friends trying to do something you already know how to do, what are you going to do?

For younger children, call parents ahead of time and ask them what their child can do well (comb hair, dry dishes, and so on). Parents, of course, don't need to go through this step. Then allow each child to demonstrate his skill to the others. Encourage the others to imitate him. Praise individuals who successfully follow the "teacher's" example. Be sure to provide appropriate materials (combs, shoelaces, washcloths).

You could also have each child tell his favorite story (small children can bring picture books they have memorized). You can specify stories that meet your lesson's theme—pioneer, Bible, and so on. Most children are proud of their memorization successes, and all love to hear stories. This is a sure way to get positive feedback for youngsters. Make sure, however, that the stories they choose are fairly short.

To Tell the Truth

This is an old traditional game that adults love as well as children. It works best with larger groups. You can play it often, but you should need to discuss it only once, after the first time. Pass out index cards and pencils, then have each child write down three sentences, each briefly summarizing an experience he has had that no one else in the room knows about. Scatter the children around the room and allow them time to write. Collect cards and bring the group back together. Quickly select an interesting statement and three children (one of them must be the person who wrote the statement) to go outside the room with you. Read the statement to the three participants and explain that two of them must invent a believable tale based on the statement, trying to fool the audience. The true author will tell the whole story as it really happened. Bring the three tellers back into the room and explain the rules to everyone else. They are to listen to the three stories. Each of the listeners will then get a chance to ask any of the tellers one question about the story. Ask them to show, by raise of hands, how many believed in the first story, second story, third story. Then reveal the true author. Keep selecting statements until everyone has had a chance to be in a trio of tellers. (Note: If you like, you can ask them to select stories centering on a specific theme to support your lesson.)

Processing questions: Why was this game so much fun? How many of you learned something new about somebody else today? Those of you whose stories were picked: Did you feel the least bit scared about everybody hearing them? Why? How do you feel now? Sometimes we feel a bit anxious when we tell something about ourselves. We're afraid people won't like us. But what really happens when we share ourselves?

For younger children, have each child pick an animal he would like to be. Bring a child up and ask him what animal he chose. Then have him pantomime things he would like to do if he were his animal. Encourage the other children to guess what he is doing and why this makes him want to be the animal. You might start things off by suggesting the first action. ("He's flying. He loves to be a bird because he can fly way up high in the sky.") Encourage the actor to do several things so the others can learn more about his animal. Feature each child in this manner.

EXPRESSING LOVE

When your children feel comfortable sharing themselves with each other, they are ready to learn different ways of expressing love and approval. Groups that begin with friendly relationships can plunge directly into deep waters with such exercises as I Love You Because . . . and If I Never Saw You Again. These kinds of activities are rewarding, and every group of children should experience them eventually.

But if your children started out on a low rung of the Love Ladder, begin with indirect games: Job Recommendation, Nonverbal Charades, Mailbox, and Renaissance Painter. Even though your children may have improved considerably since you began introducing structured experiences, their relationships are still new and fragile. Resist the temptation to speed ahead on a direct "I love you" track. They may not be ready. Be prepared to retreat if they exhibit chronic signs of anxiety—nervous joking, frustration, destructive behavior. The following games harmonize with the Savior's most important message: Love one another. All of them can augment any lesson that touches on this theme.

I Love You Because . . .

For older children and adults, simply write the name of each person on a separate sheet of paper. The papers rotate around the group, each person writing down why they love the person whose name is on the paper. When everyone has written on all papers, someone can read the papers out loud to the group.

When doing this with younger children, prepare several smiley-face badges of different colors. Bring children to your side in pairs. Have one child complete the following sentence, facing the other child: "I love you because . . ." Ask the other child if that made him happy. If so, allow him to choose a smiley-face badge and put it on his partner. Then let the second child complete the same sentence for his partner and receive his badge. Keep switching roles until both children have two or three badges. Bring up another pair and repeat the process until all children have their badges. This can be done several times every session by mixing up different pairs.

After the activity, discuss their feelings: How did you feel when you heard the nice things people said about you? Why? How do you feel about _____ (Hal, Pat, Con, and so on)? Do you think that saying nice things about other people makes them feel as good as you feel when they say nice things about you? Why? What are some ways we can tell people we love them?

A variation on this theme is the Sweetheart Kid. Once a week, choose a "child of the day." Have a cutout heart for that child. Solicit from the others several one- or two-word statements describing that child, and write those words on the heart. Pin the heart to the child's shirt for the day.

Mailbox

This is a great indirect way for family members and older children to express approval for one another. Tell your children they will be writing letters to each other, but first they must have mailboxes to receive them. Pass out mailbox materials (shoeboxes, scissors, paper, ribbon, glue) and provide a time limit for completion. Line up finished boxes along a table, or scatter them throughout the room on chairs. Explain to the children that they will each write letters to *everyone* else. Their goal is to make each person they write to feel good about himself. Lead a short discussion on effective ways to express approval, using the guideline sheet below. For groups that can read well, provide a copy of the sheet for each person; otherwise, display a poster showing one or two key words for each rule. Suggested poster words are italicized in the guideline sheet.

Write a message to each person in the class / family. The purpose of this message is to make each person you write to feel good about himself. Use the following guidelines to help you write the message:
1. Be *specific:* Say, "I like the way you smile at everyone when you come in," rather than, "I like your personality."
2. Write a *special* message to fit that person, not about something that a lot of other people have.
3. Tell this person his real *strength or success* and why you are glad to be with him.
4. Be *personal:* Use his name. Say things like "I feel . . ." or "I like . . ." as much as you can.

After they finish each letter, they are to sign it (unless they really don't want to), seal it in an envelope, and deliver it to the right mailbox. They are to do this for everyone.

I suggest that you begin by delivering a letter you have written to each of your children. Reading what you have written will help them understand the elements of specific approval that you've just discussed. They will also enjoy reading why you admire them.

Then spread the children out and pass out guideline sheets, paper, cardboard barriers, pencils or pens, and envelopes. Give the children enough time to write and deliver their letters. When all have delivered their mail, let them open their letters and read quietly to themselves. Start processing when everyone has had a chance to read at least one or two letters.

Processing questions: How do you feel after reading your letters? How do you feel about yourself? about the others in the room? As you were writing each of your letters, did you find yourself gradually admiring the person more and more? Why do you suppose this happened? A lot of researchers were surprised when they conducted a big experiment with young people your age. They found that people who praised others all the time felt good and happy about themselves. They liked just about everyone. What are some of the things Jesus said that explain why this happens?

Another idea for the mailbox is to assign secret friends to deliver messages and small care packages to another person. Challenge them to keep their identities a secret. After two or three weeks, let each person guess who his secret admirer was.

Families can continue the mailboxes permanently. Encourage family members to jot down brief messages to each other when they see someone else do an admirable thing. Children who can't write can make little picture presents or deliver small tokens such as flower petals or beautiful pebbles. The activity shouldn't die if Mom and Dad keep the fire burning by delivering mail on a continual basis. These notes will become your children's most prized mementos, and a source of encouragement throughout their lives.

Nonverbal Charades

This exercise helps older children become sensitive to the way they express affection nonverbally. Even conservative scholars agree that only 35 percent of our communication consists of spoken words. The rest comes from tone of voice, eye contact, expression, gestures, posture—powerful wordless communicators. More liberal estimates go so far as to say that 95 percent of our interaction is nonverbal. Given a choice between contradictory messages (words say one thing, eyes say another), we will generally believe the nonverbal statement. (This may explain the perfectly

charming hostess who somehow always makes me
feel like the Neanderthal Woman.) Many times we unwittingly send the wrong message nonverbally, even
when we mean well. We can help our children avoid
frustration by developing an awareness of their
nonverbal communication.

Randomly pair up the children by numbering them
off or drawing names, or by some other method.
Spread the couples around the room. Give each pair a
paper grocery sack and each child a Charade Sheet,
Instruction Sheet, and pencil. Be sure one child gets
Instructions A, the other Instructions B.

Charade Sheet

Round 1 A _____   Round 5 A _____
        B _____   B _____
        C _____   C _____

Round 2 A _____   Round 6 A _____
        B _____   B _____
        C _____   C _____

Round 3 A _____   Round 7 A _____
        B _____   B _____
        C _____   C _____

Round 4 A _____
        B _____
        C _____

Instructions A

"We're having a party. Are you coming?"

Round 1: Say the above sentence three times with a
    sack over your head. Each time, say it with the
    following attitudes, in the order given below:

     A. You don't want him to come
     B. You really want him to come
     C. You couldn't care less

Round 3: Say the above sentence silently to yourself with the sack over your head. Say it nonverbally to your partner with your hands:
     A. You couldn't care less
     B. You don't want him to come
     C. You really want him to come

Round 5: Say the above sentence silently again, expressing it nonverbally with your face:
     A. You really want him to come
     B. You don't want him to come
     C. You couldn't care less

Instructions B

"We're having a party. Are you coming?"

Round 1: Say the above sentence three times with a sack over your head. Each time, say it with the following attitudes, in the order given below:
     A. You really want him to come
     B. You couldn't care less
     C. You don't want him to come

Round 3: Say the above sentence silently to yourself with the sack over your head. Say it nonverbally to your partner with your hands:
     A. You don't want him to come
     B. You really want him to come
     C. You couldn't care less

Round 5: Say the above sentence silently again, expressing it nonverbally with your face:
     A. You couldn't care less
     B. You really want him to come
     C. You don't want him to come

Point to a poster or blackboard with the following written on it:

"We're having a party. Are you coming?"
1. You can't stand him. You don't want him to come.
2. You don't know him. You couldn't care less.
3. You like him a lot. You really want him to come.

Explain that the children are going to experiment with different ways to say the sentence. Explain what *nonverbal* means—ways of telling people how we feel about them without words. Inform them you will tell them what to do for each round.

Run through each round, allowing two minutes per round (one minute per partner). Go through the first round slowly, checking to make sure they understand what they are to do. The next rounds should go rapidly. You can read the following directions for each round:

Round 1: Decide which one of you will be Number A and who will be Number B. Number A, read over the instructions for Round 1, then put the sack over your head. Keep your body straight and stiff. Say the sentence with Attitude A. Number B, write down on your Charade Sheet what you think his attitude was. Write it under "Round 1, A." Do the other two attitudes. (Pause long enough for them to say both sentences. Reveal the correct order.) Now it's Number B's turn. Say your sentences as you are told in your instruction sheet, with the sack on. (Pause. Reveal correct order.)

Round 2: Number A, put the sack on again. Say the same sentence, but this time find three different ways to say you like your partner, using only your tone of voice. Number B, pick the one you liked the best and mark it on your Charade Sheet under Round 2. Tell your partner which one you chose and why. Now it's Number B's turn.

Round 3: Number A gets the sack again. This time try to express your attitude using your hands only, saying the sentence silently to yourself with the sack on. (Pause.) Number B try it. (Reveal correct orders.)

Round 4: Number A, take the paper sack for the last time. Find three different ways to say you like your partner using only your hands, without saying the sentence. (Pause.) Number B, pick the best one. Now Number B gets the sack. (Pause for B to do exercise.)

Round 5: Lay down your paper sacks. Number A, keep your body rigid. You cannot speak out loud. Now you are going to express your attitude with your face. (Give them time to express and mark on sheets.) Number B try it. (Reveal orders.)

Round 6: Number A, find three different ways to say you like your partner using only your face. Number B, choose the best one. (Give them time to express and mark sheets.) Number B's turn.

Round 7: Now you will have two minutes to practice for a contest. Combine good ways of saying the sentence as though you really liked each other. You can change the sentence if you like. You will be judged on the following:
A. Do you seem to *really* like each other?
B. Did you say it to each other with your faces? your hands? your voices?

After they've had two minutes to practice, bring everyone together into a semicircle. Give each pair a chance to demonstrate their charade in front of the group. Assign different people to watch hands, faces, voices. Ask the group to vote by raise of hands on the pair that did the best job with their faces. Next, vote on hands, then voices. Then vote on overall sincerity.

Ask the children to just think about the following questions: This was just a game, but did you feel bad anyway when your partner told you about the party as if he didn't want you to come? How did you feel every time he said the sentence as if he really wanted you to come? How do you treat other people nonverbally? How are you making them feel?

Next, discuss out loud these questions: Which nonverbal ways of communicating seemed easier than others? Which were harder? Why? What have you learned from this exercise? The Savior once said, "Do unto others as you would have them do unto you." How does this commandment apply to the way we talk to other people?

Six- and seven-year-olds can play this game if you can overcome reading and writing difficulties. I've found success by substituting faces for words to portray attitudes (☺☺☹). I found it necessary to check each child's charade sheet after each sentence during Round 1 to help them get the idea. After that trial, however, it goes quite swiftly. These younger children generally show more imagination and have more fun when they invent nonverbal expressions.

Job Recommendation

This activity appeals to children over seven years old. Divide them into pairs. Tell them they will take turns pretending they are going to a job interview. Their partners will help them by giving recommendations to the boss. Tell the job seekers to give their partners three pieces of information:
1. What kind of job I want to have
2. Two things I do well
3. A recent accomplishment or success

Give partners two to three minutes to prepare their recommendations. Older children should be given paper and pencils for notes. Gather the group up and have them listen to the recommendations (partners are to stand together in front of the group) and vote for the best presentation. If a recommendation seems superior, have them discuss what made it so. Then have the partners reverse roles and repeat the game.

Processing questions: What was harder, telling somebody your strengths, or telling other people about somebody else's strengths? Why? After you recommended your partner, how did you feel about him? How did you feel about yourself? When you were seeking a job, how did you feel after your partner recommended you to the boss? Do you think you might have felt differently if you had had to talk to the boss by yourself? Why? What can we do when we want to make people feel more confident and happy about themselves? What can we do when we need confidence and courage from someone else?

You can vary this theme to fit your lesson. Youngsters can, for example, recommend each other for mission calls, baptism, or parenthood.

For three- to five-year-olds, bring a child to the front. Put your arm around him and tell him specifically several reasons why you admire him. Tell him you love him for what he is. Hug him and kiss him on the forehead. Have each of the other children come up and repeat the same actions for this child. Encourage them to think of their own reasons for loving him, and to hug him. Feature every child in this manner.

Another idea for little ones is to have a child pretend he is his favorite flower. Encourage the children to walk around the flower and admire it any way they like, such as patting his cheek, saying, "Ooh-aah, how beautiful!" and so on. Ask the children to decide who loves the flower the most. Pick one child to take the flower "home" (back to sit with him). You can feature

all your children this way in one session, but I suggest
spreading it out over several times, perhaps doing it
before every home evening or Primary lesson. It will be
something they will eagerly look forward to.

Renaissance Painter

This is another indirect way to creatively express
approval. Try it on seven- to eleven-year-olds. Explain
to your children that they will be painting a picture
Renaissance style. Renaissance artists very often
painted people they admired or liked a great deal.
They tried to emphasize the quality they liked. One
man in a picture, for example, would be painted with a
twinkle in his eye because he laughed so much. A
woman might be wearing a soft, flowing dress because
she was so gentle. The children will each be painting a
picture of someone in the room. They must find a way
to paint a picture that will tell the rest of the group
what they admire about that person. Have the children draw names out of a hat and tell them to keep
their names a secret. Pass out paint materials and
allow each child to complete and then show his drawing. Encourage the rest of the group to guess who is in
the picture and what his admirable trait is. Have the
artist explain his painting.

Processing questions: What was the hardest part of
this activity? Were any of you surprised by the things
someone admired about you? How do you feel about
the person who painted your picture? How do you feel
about the person you painted? What are some other
ways we can tell other people how much they mean to
us?

You can try other media, such as clay, ink, or finger
paints. Or instead of portraits, have them paint objects
that symbolize the positive feelings they have for their
models (such as a flower, tree, house, or bird).

For younger children, have them make and decorate hearts. If they can write, have them write, "I love

you, _____ (name of other child). Love, _____ (his own name)." Have them give their hearts away to each other.

Smiley Game

This is a nonverbal exercise for small children. They have a lot of fun with this one. Tell your children they are going on a special field trip. They must try to get as many "good" points as they can during their walk. Points count for the whole group. The children earn points by getting people they see to respond to their actions. They cannot say anything. Various responses from people have different point values: A smile equals 5 points, a wave equals 8 points, and verbal response equals 10 points. Explain what you want the children to do: "See how many people you can get to smile, wave, or say 'hello' without you saying a word." If you have eight or more children, divide them into subgroups of four or five, assigning each group a supervisor who will record points. Have groups compete against each other for points. Lead the group outside. As the children practice this Smiley Game you should record points and guide your children away from using verbal contact with strangers. ("Oh-oh! You said something! Try to say the same thing without words.")

After you return, tally points and challenge them to get a higher score the next time. This is a game you can play several times. Discuss the following questions: What did people do when you smiled or waved? Why? How do you feel when people smile at you? People feel good when you tell them you like them, even when you say it without words. How many of you want to make each other happy? How are you going to do that?

With older children, you can get an adventurous child to solicit responses to negative expressions (frown, smirk, stick out tongue), while everyone else watches. Be sure to get the same individual to solicit positive responses as well. Points should not be awarded for the negative expressions.

If I Never Saw You Again

This is an advanced activity for older children that should be done only after they have participated in several other games in this section. By the time you get to this point, they should feel completely comfortable about saying "I love you." Do not run this exercise with children under seven years old: The thought of losing a loved one is too real and terrifying for them.

Tell your children to pretend that this is the last time they will ever see each other again. (You might want to suggest a scenario such as a fatal car accident or a sudden disaster that separates everyone. Explain that they will have a few minutes to think about what they want to say to every other person. They can take notes if they want. Distribute copies of the following sheet and ask them to use it as a guideline for what they say to each other.

If I Never Saw You Again . . .

I would feel_____ because _____.
You mean a great deal to me because _____.
I would miss your_____. I want you to know something I've never told you before: _____
_____. I will always remember how you_____.
I want you to know that I_____you.

Spread the children out, seat them facing walls, and pass out paper and pencils. Give them time to think about their feelings. Station half the group in different parts of the room, sitting down. These children will always stay where they are throughout the exercise. Have each of the remaining children find a seated partner and sit in front of him. Give them two to four minutes to talk to each other about their feelings, based on the guideline sheet. Then have the mobile half of the group rotate to other partners. Repeat the process until each person has conversed with every-one else.

Processing questions: How do you feel about this exercise? Which parts were the hardest to talk about? Are you glad you talked your feelings out with each other? Why? Are your friendships better now than they were an hour ago? What does this tell us about friendships and how we can strengthen them?

4

Leadership Skills:

"I Want to Treat You Well"

While the Israelites were camped in the desert, a young man ran up to Moses and breathlessly told of upstarts who prophesied among the people. Joshua begged his master to forbid such usurping of power. Instead of rising with rage, however, Moses taught an important lesson to Joshua, who would one day lead the vast multitude of Israel as general and prophet: "Enviest thou for my sake? would God that all the Lord's people were prophets and that the Lord would put his spirit upon them!" (Numbers 11:29.)

The ideal for any group of God's children is for each individual to be a strong, righteous leader, united together with the others into one powerful wedge of action. In all, there are nearly fifteen leadership functions, including: initiating actions, keeping the group oriented to its goals, giving and seeking information, evaluating information, clarifying what others have said, coordinating various opinions, testing for consensus, suggesting procedures, recording what is being said and done, encouraging others to participate, delegating responsibility, relieving tension, supporting other contributions. Very few people exercise all functions in a single meeting, though it is desirable to acquire as many of these skills as possible. If we were to study a highly productive group, we would probably find these functions evenly divided among group members, each individual typically contributing three or four leadership qualities. Training seminars for adults often help group members identify the functions they usually fall into when they meet in a group. Seminar participants are also given opportunities to practice additional skills to give them flexibility and the capacity to fill in for others when needed.

Though children are not ready to memorize all the different leadership functions, you, as an adult supervisor, should keep them in the back of your mind. Try to give every child opportunities to practice all functions. The remaining exercises in this book are designed to help children develop these various skills. They are treated in ascending order of difficulty.

SELF-EVALUATION

A five-year-old boy in one of my classes habitually yanked on a little girl's hair. Exasperated, I exclaimed, "Bobby, don't you know that hurts Susan every time you pull on her hair?" He looked at me with big, wondering eyes. "If you keep hurting her," I continued, "she won't like you anymore." His eyes grew even bigger with surprise. He looked genuinely sorry and proved it by hugging his victim. He answered my question without saying a word. He really didn't know he was hurting Susan! What is more, he didn't realize what his actions were doing to his relationship with his friend.

Most people—children and adults alike—are not aware of what they do with each other. This is certainly true in group settings. We may have vague feelings about how others respond to us, but we hardly ever stop to analyze what we do to promote such responses. Before concentrating on specific areas of leadership, your children need to know how they are currently acting and to feel motivated to improve themselves. Before trying any of the games in this chapter, you will need to spend some discussion time defining and labeling different kinds of behavior. This lesson can be anywhere from five to forty-five minutes in length, depending on your style of teaching, the ages of your children, and their current profile (based on the questionnaire in chapter 2). Generally, it takes longer if you are used to open discussion, if your children are older, or if they have fewer leadership skills.

Check your answers to the leadership and listening questions in your questionnaire. A group with good leadership skills is not dominated by a single individual. Contributions to discussions should be evenly divided among everyone, each taking turns to listen to everyone else. Smaller children in the family may not lead out as often, but their ideas should be sought out and considered. All children should be confident about asserting themselves, and feel comfortable about working on group tasks.

Your discussion on behavior should contain the following four elements:

1. Define Leadership

You may want your children to brainstorm different aspects of leadership, but guide them to the following conclusions:

There are many different ways to be a leader. A leader is brave, humble, gives and asks directions, makes plans, works hard, sets a good example, helps and loves other people.

A great leader helps those around him become leaders too. He encourages them to give advice. He gives them responsibility. He tries to make them so good at leading that he can go away and not worry about things getting done.

Jesus was a great leader. It's always a good idea to illustrate good behavior by examining a great personality. Analyze Jesus' leadership. Discuss specific instances when he demonstrated all the qualities of great leadership.

2. *Define Behavior Types*

During this part of the lesson, associate pleasing behavior with desirable role models, and destructive behavior with unpopular ones. The following is a list of suggested role models with different themes. Use your imagination to come up with a combination that your youngsters can relate to with enthusiasm.

	(Animals)	(Star Wars)	(Bible)
Achiever	Busy Beaver	Luke Skywalker Princess Leia	Moses
Peacemaker	Oscar Otter	R2-D2	Aaron
Wreaker	Blubber Baboon	Darth Vader	Pharaoh
Dropout	Dead Worm	Android	Egyptians

You may want to show pictures of your chosen role characters, especially to small children, and ask them to describe their feelings for each of the roles. Define the roles:

Achiever: A leader. Gives ideas, makes suggestions, decides what to do, and works to get it done.

Peacemaker: A leader. Encourages others to participate, praises and supports ideas, makes peace during arguments.

Wreaker: Never listens to other people, makes fun of suggestions, throws temper tantrums, gets mad, yells, refuses to cooperate, never lets anyone else plan things or give directions.

Dropout: Never says or does anything. Just sits there.

3. *Provide Reinforcement*

Give the children a scenario to act out, with a specific role for each to play. If you have more than four children in your group have the remaining ones guess which actor is playing which part. I've found that little children (ages three to five) need something tangible to remind them of their roles—posters around their necks, simple props, or costumes. It is very important to assign children roles that do not typify their normal behavior, particularly when it comes to undesirable behavior. For example, if you have a shy child who hardly ever participates, give him an Achiever role or even Wreaker, but never Dropout.

Help the children act out their roles ("What does Skywalker think of to save the planet?" "Oops, Dead Worm isn't supposed to say anything." "Does Moses ever yell at anybody?" "I thought Blubber Baboon never helped anyone.") They'll get the hang of it as they go deeper into the scenario. The scenario should be a failure—if Wreaker and Dropout never cooperate, the leaders should be impotent to fulfill their roles. This fact should be discussed: *Everyone needs to be a leader if we are all going to succeed.* Then allow the same actors to be themselves and reenact the scenario as though they were all leaders trying to solve a common problem. Give everyone a chance to role-play. The following are ideas for scenarios with various themes:

(Animals:) Humans left a campfire burning in your forest. How are you going to save your home?

(Star Wars:) The Empire is about to blow up Princess Leia's home planet with its super machine. Luke Skywalker and R2-D2 aren't strong enough to lift the trap door to their ship. Their only hope is to get into their ship and blow out the missile timing device.

(Bible:) Moses must get his people out of Egypt so they can worship God in their own country. The Egyptians are suffering terribly from all the plagues God has sent against them.

4. Run a Self-evaluation Exercise

This step is needed only for older children (age seven and above) who have begun to act out consistent

Role Worksheet

Achiever	Peacemaker
Wreaker	Dropout

roles. Assign a very simple task, observe and report total group performance, and have each person privately fill out a questionnaire. The six tasks suggested at the end of this section are all simple ranking exercises appropriate for this type of self-evaluation. Choose one of these six Group Ranking Tasks and make enough copies for each child to have one and also for each group to have an extra. Allow children to work on their lists individually before forming groups, then have them join together in ranking the items as a group. This exercise gives you the opportunity to observe their behavior while they are engrossed in a task.

If you have them divided into more than one group (each group should have about four or five members), enlist adult help to observe other groups. While the children are working through the exercise, mark the Role Worksheet as follows: Every time anyone speaks, put a slash mark in the box that best describes that comment. At the end of the task, place a large black circle in the Dropout box for each person who did not contribute very much.

At the end of the exercise, let the groups explain why they made their choices, then pass out My Behavior questionnaires. Included here are two questionnaires at different reading levels. I suggest you read the questions out loud, giving the children time to mark their answers after each. This will help those who may have difficulty understanding the questions. Emphasize that no one will be reading their answers; the sheet is for their own private use only. Use the key to discuss what their answers mean. Encourage your children to honestly evaluate themselves.

My Behavior

(Advanced Questionnaire)

Rank yourself on the following:
1. How much did you talk compared to everyone else?
   (Never talked / Equal / Did most of the talking)
2. How often did you try to get other people to talk?
   (Never / Sometimes / All the time)
3. How often did you lose your temper?
   (Never / Sometimes / A lot)
4. Who in your group did very little to help? What did you do about it?
5. Did anyone argue with anyone else during the task? What did you do about it?
6. How would you rate your leadership during this task?

1	2	3	4	5
Poor	Fair	Average	Good	Excellent

7. Write the names of those you worked with, and beside each one put what you think of the ideas

they contributed during the task.
(Terrible / Poor / Average / Good / Excellent)

Key: Leaders should score equal on #1, high on #2 and #3. They attempted to involve shy people (#4) and to settle arguments (#5). They gave high ratings on #7 (leaders respect everyone's ideas). If all of these are rated as described above, the children are justified in marking high on #6. If not, they need to reevaluate themselves.

My Behavior

(Simple Questionnaire)

Circle the words that answer the questions:
1. During the game I talked (A lot / Sometimes / Never)
2. Everyone talked a lot (Yes / No)
3. I got mad (A lot / Sometimes / Never)
4. I liked to hear what others said (Yes / No)
5. I think somebody in my group is stupid (Yes / No)
6. I didn't want to talk (Yes / No)
7. I praised somebody (Yes / No)
8. I said what I thought was right (Yes / No)
9. My group made dumb choices (Yes / No)
10. Somebody in my group never said anything (Yes / No)

Key

Achiever:
1. A lot
2. Yes
3. Never
4. Yes
5. No
6. No
8. Yes
9. No
10. No

(If they circled "no" on #2 or "yes" on #10, they are not leaders because they did not help someone else be part of the game.)

Peacemaker:	3. Yes	Wreaker	5. Yes
	4. Yes	(cont.)	7. No
	5. No		9. Yes
	7. Yes		
	10. No		
		Dropout:	1. Never
Wreaker:	3. A lot		6. Yes
	4. No		8. No

After your children have evaluated themselves, show the results of your observations. Talk about general strengths and weaknesses. ("You all gave many opinions, but nobody seemed to be listening to anyone else," or, "One person seemed to be doing all the talking.") Talk about specific instances during the game which you think were destructive, leaving out names. ("I remember somebody telling another to shut up. I marked that down as Wreaker.") Let the children talk about what they thought needed to be improved and how they could have done the exercise better. Emphasize that it is all right to disagree. In fact, disagreement is healthy, a sign of thought and creativity. It's *how* we disagree that counts. Encourage them to say, "I disagree because . . ." (a Leader statement), not "That's a dumb idea" (a Wreaker statement).

At this point I like to give the children a chance to improve themselves, knowing that I am marking down their statements. I pick another group ranking task and assign a child to observe the group alongside me, marking a sheet like mine. I let him give his report before I do. There is no point in having the children fill out another behavior questionnaire, since they already know what the "right" answers are.

GROUP RANKING TASKS

Lost on the Moon

Your spaceship has just crash-landed on the dark side of the moon. You were scheduled to rendezvous with a mother ship two hundred miles away on the lighted surface of the moon, but the rough landing has ruined your ship and destroyed all the equipment on board except for the fifteen items listed below. Your crew's survival depends on reaching the mother ship, so you must choose the most critical items in terms of their importance for survival. Place a number 1 by the most important, number 2 by the second most important, and so on through number 15.

____ Box of matches ____ Food concentrate
____ Parachute silk ____ Self-inflating life raft
____ Five gallons of water ____ Magnetic compass
____ Fifty feet of nylon rope ____ Signal flares
____ Solar-powered portable heating unit
____ Two .45-caliber pistols
____ One case of dehydrated milk
____ Two 100-pound tanks of oxygen
____ Stellar map (of the moon's constellations)
____ First-aid kit containing injection needles
____ Solar-powered FM receiver-transmitter

Pioneer Family Survival

Your family is traveling to Zion across the wilderness. You've had many delays, waiting for Grandpa Clark to join you from England, building your wagon, finding oxen to pull your wagon, and fighting off Indians. Now you've reached high mountain country just as the first winter snow begins to fall. On top of that, your extra cattle have been stolen. You must decide which things you will leave behind as the going gets desperate. Number the most important thing first (1) and so on, numbering the least important thing last (15).

____ Extra clothing ____ Oil lamps
____ Blankets   ____ Hand organ
____ Seeds   ____ Lard

____ Family Bible	____ Pet dog
____ Pots and pans	____ Table
____ Water	____ Rifle
____ Dried bacon	____ Fiddle
____ Flour	

Occupational Prestige

How important are these jobs? Rank them. Place the number 1 in front of the job you think is the most important. Keep numbering them, placing a 15 next to the least important job.

____ Novelist	____ Newspaper reporter
____ Policeman	____ Banker
____ Judge	____ Lawyer
____ Farmer	____ Senator
____ Inventor	____ Salesman
____ Schoolteacher	____ Dentist
____ Cowboy	____ Actor
____ Doctor	

Qualities of a Friend

Which qualities are the most important for a friend to have? Rank them from 1 to 15 (1 being the most important trait).

____ Good-looking	____ Cheerful
____ Popular	____ Well dressed
____ Thoughtful	____ Fun
____ Encouraging	____ Caring
____ Spiritual	____ Intelligent
____ Trustworthy	____ Honest
____ Sharing	____ Helpful
____ Rich	

LEADING AND SUPPORTING

There are two types of games in this section. The first three games (Lincoln Logging Company, Maze, and My Yard) teach children how to be formal leaders and attentive followers. Formal leaders are people who are officially responsible for the completion of a task, telling others how to reach their common goal. I have discovered that these games are especially great for shy children. You will be amazed at the transformation! They will light up with sudden joy and confidence as others look to them for guidance. I have often thrilled as thumb-suckers and timid onlookers rise up to happy levels of self-assurance. In these exercises, children take turns being formal leaders. Plan to have your more timid youngsters lead halfway through (don't put them first or last). Lincoln Logging Company is particularly popular among the children I have taught.

The other games do not have formal leaders, but stress the idea of group cooperation, wherein everyone is a leader. They are designed to illustrate the advantage of pooling resources to achieve greater success for each person.

Lincoln Logging Company

Children of all ages love this game. For younger children, you can simply substitute large colored blocks of various shapes for Lincoln Logs. If you have enough children, divide them into competitive groups of four to six members. A single group can compete against time. Give each child a sealed envelope labeled A, B, C, D, or E containing a diagram of a Lincoln Log design. Each blueprint should be different. (See accompanying example.)

Give Child A a pile of Lincoln Logs and instruct him to pass them out equally among his crew, excluding himself. Then tell Child A to open the envelope and direct his crew in building the structure without show-

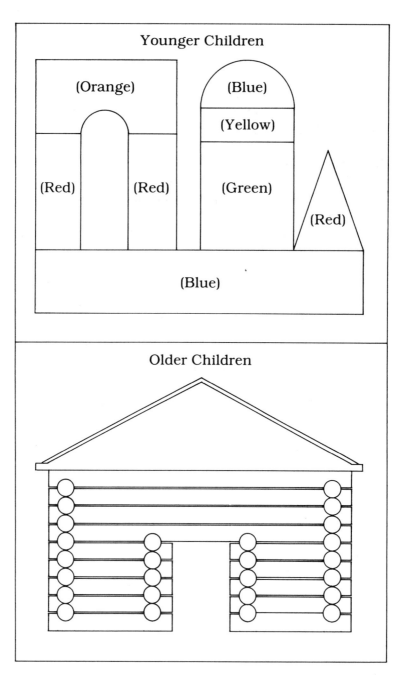

Lincoln Log Blueprint Examples

ing them the blueprint. Allow each person in turn to open an envelope and direct the group. The winning group is the one that completes all building projects first. A single group can strive to improve their time with each new set of building projects.

Processing questions: What did you have to do to complete your structure? Suppose the foreman decided not to tell you how to build? What would happen? Suppose one of you decided not to listen and follow directions—what would happen to the building? Throughout all our lives we will be part of groups with important goals—families, Church organizations, business work groups. Sometimes we will be the official leaders; sometimes we will be helping someone else be an official leader. What have we learned from this game that will help us be better leaders and supporters?

To vary the theme, you can have the children build something from your home evening or Primary lesson, such as a temple (modern or ancient), home, world, city, or map. Or use a different medium: clay, candy, boxes, household utensils, Legos, Tinkertoys, wooden craft sticks.

Maze

This works well for six- to eleven-year-olds. Divide your children into pairs and instruct partners to decide who will be the leader and who will be the follower. Each leader receives a blindfold. Instruct the leaders to take their partners to the entrance of the maze room and blindfold their followers before entering. After followers have been blindfolded, give each leader a maze diagram (see accompanying illustration). Line the pairs up at one end of the maze. Have each leader direct his follower verbally through the maze. Allow each follower to reach the end before letting another pair begin the maze. As they proceed, record the leader's name and the time it took to get through the maze. Record how many times the follower touched a

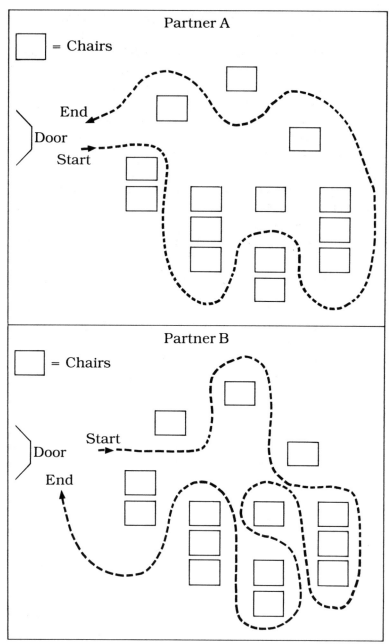

Maze Diagram

wall or chair ("hits"). Assemble the entire group in the original room and announce the time and number of hits for each pair. There are no "winners" in this game. Reverse roles and give the new leaders different diagrams. Repeat the game.

You may want to build your processing questions on lesson material about following the prophet or the Lord. Other questions may include: What was more difficult for you, giving directions or following directions blindfolded? Why? When you were watching other people trying to go through the maze, what problems did you notice? How could these be solved? Sometimes we are asked to trust in an official leader because he has information we don't have. How can we be sure to reach our goal? What are some things we can do to make ourselves more clearly understood when we are giving directions?

If space is limited, a maze can be represented on a sheet of paper and the task revised so that the blindfolded partner draws a continuous line from start to finish, avoiding obstacles on the paper, by following verbal directions of the leader. Or the maze could be a scriptural journey: a path through a mountain pass, a nighttime spying mission on the Philistines, Jonah finding Nineveh. It could be an abstract journey through temptations, repentance, or earthly ordinances.

My Yard

My Yard helps three- to six-year-olds experience leadership. Place one child behind a barricaded desk or table so that other children cannot see over the top. Give the child a simple picture of a yard with various items arranged in a certain way. Instruct the child to keep his picture hidden from everyone else. Give each of the remaining children a large replica of an item in the picture. Instruct the group to assemble a picture on a bulletin board or wall with their items.

After they have arranged the picture, let one child from the group approach the desk and ask if the "big" picture is the same as the "little" picture. The child with the small picture can answer either yes or no. If he says no, the group must assemble the picture once more. Again, the child sitting at the desk reveals whether the order is correct. If it is not, he can tell which items need to be moved, but does not tell where they should be moved. After the children reassemble the picture, the child at the desk again indicates correctness. If the big picture is still wrong, the child at the desk may tell the group where to move the pieces. During this game, you will probably need to whisper instructions to the barricaded leader.

Processing questions: What would have happened if one of you had part of the picture and decided not to play? What happens when everyone does his part in a group effort? If I had never let your leader give good directions, would you have finished it as fast? When we are telling people how to do something, what do we need to do to make sure they understand what we want?

You can make a puzzle that suits your lesson, such as a word strip scramble, creation days, Jerusalem, and so on.

Block Market

This is another popular all-age game that sparks laughter as well as cooperation. If you have more than five children, divide them into competitive groups. If not, your children can compete against a stopwatch.

Assuming you have five children, give each of them five blocks of a single color (that is, five red blocks or five yellow blocks). No two children should have the same color of blocks. Outline the goal as follows: Each person should end up with one block of each color; no person should have more than one block of the same color. Groups are allowed to give and take at will. The group that completes the assignment first is the winner. If you only have one group, have them race against the clock, striving to improve their time. Let them play this game at least three times.

Processing questions: How did you manage to get the blocks you needed? What does *cooperation* mean? Suppose one person had decided not to cooperate— what would have happened to everybody else? When we are working with other people, how can we cooperate with them so we all get what we want?

A more challenging version for older children is to give the group different directions for each round—for example, they can't talk during Round 1, they can only give or take blocks from one other person during Round 2, they can talk and give freely during Round 3. Instead of blocks they could exchange items mentioned in your home evening or Primary lesson, such as flowers, moons, planets, family members (each person trying to form a complete family), or pictures of early Church leaders.

Puzzling

Young children love puzzles! Try this on your three- to six-year-olds. Randomly divide them into groups of five or six members, or, if you only have a few children, plan to have them race against the clock. Arrange the children around a table or large space on the floor. Give each child a piece of a giant puzzle. (Give extra pieces to older or quicker youngsters.) Do not allow them to fit pieces until you give the word. (A giant puzzle can be made by gluing a poster to a large piece of cardboard and cutting it into jigsaw pieces with a mat knife. I've found that I need three or four puzzles on hand to satisfy the children's enthusiasm.)

Explain the rules:

1. The goal is to finish the puzzle before the other groups finish theirs (or for one group to finish the puzzle as fast as they can).
2. Only the person holding his puzzle piece can put it into place. If anyone grabs a piece from

somebody else, they have to start all over again (you will mix up the puzzle and redistribute pieces).

3. They may not talk.

Tell them to begin. After they complete the puzzle, announce the winning group or time, then mix up puzzle pieces and redistribute them. Repeat the game. You may want to exchange puzzles between groups. Discussion questions will be similar to those for My Yard.

You can vary this game by choosing puzzle pictures that fit a particular theme: Jesus blessing children, flowery meadows, Church leaders, or a story illustration. For older children, give each person a word or two from a scripture. Have them combine their words to make your theme verse.

Photo Memory

This is another good all-age game. Project a transparency or show a poster picturing miscellaneous items, telling your children to memorize as many of the items as they can. (Younger children should have five to ten items; older children need twenty to thirty.) Give them thirty seconds to study the pictures. Remove the poster or transparency and tell them to list or draw as many items as they can remember. They are not to talk with one another.

After enough time has elapsed, ask each child to state how many items he remembered (don't ask him *what* he saw). Form groups and tell the children to list items as a group, essentially combining everyone's list. Discuss results. Compare the highest individual score with the highest group score. If you have only one group, let each child verbally list what he has while you write the items down. Compare individual with group results.

Next, warn your children that they will see another, different picture. They will have a minute to plan their strategy for memorizing all the items in the picture as a group. If you have a younger group, suggest to them that they assign each person a section of the picture to memorize (upper right, middle, and so on). Give them time to plan. Show the new picture and process the results with the following questions: Was it easier to remember more pictures by yourself or with everybody else? Why? Did a minute of planning with each other help? Why? Can you think of times in your life when you could do better if you cooperated with other people instead of trying to do something by yourself? What can we do to make sure we get the most out of our group efforts?

This game could augment a family theme of cooperation. Use it to demonstrate how family members can reach celestial life much more easily if everyone works together as a unit.

Twin Peaks

Do you have a rambunctious group of seven- to eleven-year-olds? Challenge them with this game. Divide them into teams and take them outside. If you have a small group, put one person against everyone else. (Make sure the loner is an outgoing volunteer who can handle this activity with a sense of humor. You may want to issue a challenge: "Okay, do we have a bionic man or woman to beat everybody else?") If you have a larger group, you can divide them into three teams, each heavily outnumbering the next (perhaps two, five, and ten members).

Give each team five minutes to build a mountain as high as they can out of sand or snow. Ask a few processing questions:
1. Why did Team A end up with a bigger mountain?
2. (Directed to loner) How did you feel during this contest?

Let the loner exchange places with a member of the larger team. This time, the new loner will be working on the high mountain already built by the larger team, and the bigger team will work on the smaller mountain. Give them five minutes to build up their moun-

tains, then ask more discussion questions: Who has
got the bigger mountain? Why were you able to beat
_____ (second loner) even though you
started with a smaller peak?_____ (first
loner), how did you feel when you suddenly found
yourself with more people to help you on your peak?
_____ (second loner), how did you feel
this time compared to last time? Why? (See Photo
Memory for more questions.)

You can swing with the seasons by using a different medium such as grass clippings, autumn leaves,
clay, boxes, or building blocks (make sure there is
plenty of material available). Or have the children
build a special structure out of your lesson, such as a
wagon train, city, temple, pioneer settlement, or
house.

LISTENING AND SUPPORTING

One of the most important skills we can learn when
relating to other people is listening. Most people don't
know how to listen. We wait patiently for other people
to stop talking so we can speak our own thoughts. Not
listening attentively is the primary complaint em-
ployers have about their subordinates, and vice versa.
Group members will develop harsh feelings for one
another if they feel frustrated: "You're not listening to
me!" They may misunderstand each other's information or motives because they weren't tuned in all the
way. As you introduce these listening games, emphasize to your children that listening is the most
important skill a leader has. If they are going to be
achievers, they must be able to listen to the needs and
advice of those they lead. If they are going to be peace-
makers, they must be able to understand how and
why other people are feeling the way they are.

The first game, Are You Listening?, graphically
demonstrates how various levels of attentiveness
make us feel. The others are skill-development exer-

cises in reflective listening. By repeating back or summarizing what another person has said, we guarantee full understanding and make him feel that we respect what he is trying to say.

Are You Listening?

This game is appropriate for children of any age. Divide your children into pairs. Give each pair a paper sack and scatter them around the room.

Round 1: Child A puts the paper sack on his head. Child B is to talk about activities he enjoys the most. Give them a one-minute time limit. Reverse roles and time for another minute.

Round 2: Child A is to look at his partner but freeze his face. He is to show no expression. Child B again talks about his interests for one minute. Reverse roles for another minute.

Round 3: This time Child A is to do everything he can, short of talking, to show sincere interest in what his partner is saying. Time for a minute. Reverse roles for another minute.

Processing questions: Was it harder to talk to the paper sack? Why? How did you feel when your partner didn't seem to listen to you? How did you feel during Round 3? Why was it better? What did your partner do with his eyes to show he was listening? his face? his hands? How should we listen to people when they are trying to tell us something?

For more challenge, get the listeners to convey different attitudes for each round, such as disgust, boredom, defensiveness, or excitement. Then have the partners guess what kind of listeners they had. Or instead of using paper sacks, you can have the children turn their backs to their partners. If you want to tie the activity in with a lesson, have the children role-play special character sets during the rounds, such as Moses talking to Pharaoh, Noah talking to a neighbor, Samuel the Lamanite talking to a priest, or Joseph Smith talking to a preacher about his vision.

Repeat After Me

This is a reflective exercise for three- to six-year-olds. Divide your children into pairs. Instruct each child to pick an animal from a number of pictures shown. ("If you were an animal, what would you be?") When the children have selected their pictures, one child from each pair is to tell his partner why he would want to be the animal he chose. He should also tell everything he would do as that animal. Set a one-or two-minute time limit. Partners are told that they will have to repeat back what was said. ("Try to listen hard because you will have to tell me what he said to you.")

As the children finish their dialogues, let them come up to you as pairs. Listen to the partner repeat back what was said. When he is finished with his summary, ask the talker, "Was that what you told him?" If it is close, praise the listener. If the listener falters, encourage him ("It's hard to remember, isn't it? Listening takes a lot of work."), and have the pair go back and try it again. In any case, when the listener finally completes his assignment, let his partner reward him with a smiley badge, star, or some other token. I found it particularly effective to make listener ears—headbands with giant paper ears attached. Instruct the pairs to return to their spots and reverse roles. Repeat the game.

Processing questions: Is it hard to remember everything somebody tells you? Why? Does it help you to remember what somebody tells you when you say it back? What can you do to be a better listener?

For older children, have them think of a movie character, modern machine, or plant they would like to be. You can "congratulate" listeners with a handshake or other form of praise. You can also use a theme from your lesson by having them pick characters or objects discussed.

Switch

Switch appeals to children nine years and older.

Pair the children off and pass out name tags. Have each child write his name on the tag and put it on. Explain that they will have two minutes to exchange as much information about each other as they can, then each will switch name tags and assume his partner's identity. Encourage them to ask each other questions to clarify information. Give the pairs two minutes to talk.

Switch name tags and have everyone find a new partner to talk with. Each is to pretend to be the person whose name he is wearing. Have them switch name tags again and repeat the process three or four times or until they tire of it.

Processing questions: What was the hardest part of this exercise? If you hadn't known you were going to switch name tags, would you have listened so attentively? Why? Did you feel as though someone was truly interested in what you had to say about yourself? Why? How can we make people feel that we are sincerely listening to what they are saying?

For younger children, simplify the activity by having them exchange just one or two pieces of information (for example, "My favorite color is . . ." "I was born on . . ." "I like to eat . . .").

Mirror Me

This is another simple exercise for three- to six-year-olds. Bring a child to the front of the group. Ask him to pretend that he is either happy or sad and to act out how he feels. Ask him, "How do you feel?" After he answers, ask the other children, "How does he feel?" Get them to respond verbally, then get them to imitate his emotion: "Can you show me how he feels?" Praise individuals who successfully imitate the emotion. Then ask the child, "Why do you feel happy (sad)?" After he responds, ask the others, "Why is he happy (sad)?" Feature every child. You may want to try different kinds of emotions.

Processing questions: How do we know when somebody is listening? What can we say to show we are listening? What can we do with our faces to show we are listening?

For older children, have them take turns describing how they would act and feel in a given situation. Have the others summarize what the speaker said and felt.

Ball Toss

This is by far the most popular listening game among the eight- to eleven-year-olds I have taught. Form your children into a circle. Give one person a ball. Assign a topic to discuss; a lesson theme would be excellent. The person with the ball gives a one-sentence opinion and then tosses the ball to someone else. The next person must repeat the previous person's sentence, then give his own one-sentence thought before tossing the ball again. (Each successive child repeats only the last sentence given before adding his own.) Whenever someone "misses," stop the ball and start all over again. Start putting time limits on each person's turn. Cut the time more and more with each round.

Processing questions: Which was harder, remembering what other people said or thinking up your own opinion? Why? Compare this ball toss discussion with the regular discussions we usually have. Which discussion made you concentrate more on what other people were saying? Which one helped you form your own opinion? What can we do to make our regular conversations real "discussions," in which we all truly listen to each other before giving our own opinions?

For young children, assign them a single word to memorize, such as their favorite plant or animal. If Child A says "lion" and tosses the ball to Child B, Child B must say "lion, pig" (or whatever he has chosen as his animal) before tossing it to someone else. This game should be run rather slowly at first, so the children have time to think through their words.

5

Teamwork:

"We All Have Good Ideas"

The Lord chastised the mental laziness of a would-be translator, Oliver Cowdery: "Behold, you have not understood, you have supposed that I would give it unto you, when you took no thought save it was to ask me. But, behold, I say unto you, that you must study it out in your mind; then you must ask me if it be right." (D&C 9:7–8.) The Lord expects his children to formulate their own ideas and solutions, then seek confirmation from his Spirit.

BRAINSTORMING AND CREATIVITY

This section suggests ways to stimulate both individual and group creativity. These games are mind stretchers. During *any* brainstorming session, whether it is part of a game or real activity planning, always give time for individuals to brainstorm by themselves before opening it to the entire group. This solitary time brings several benefits. It helps to ensure participation from everyone and brings a greater number of ideas. Some people think through their ideas more carefully than others, so this time will allow them to formulate their thoughts ahead of time. If several people have independently written the same idea, it suggests a possible final solution.

If your children have trouble generating creative ideas independently, you will need to devote time to several brainstorming games. Uses Muses and Making It Up are excellent repeaters that can be played over and over again without getting old. Given a one-minute brainstorming period on a simple topic (as in Uses Muses), an average group should be able to generate at least five ideas per person. An excellent, well-oiled group should produce between ten and twenty ideas per person. When evaluating your group, don't average out scores. Base your judgment on the performance of the least productive child. Keep working on brainstorming skills until all of your children are at least on an average plane.

When you invent your own game, make sure it: (1) has a topic with unlimited possibilities, (2) allows time for individuals to brainstorm alone, (3) stimulates group brainstorming, (4) discourages judgment during the brainstorming period.

Uses Muses and Making It Up are purely brainstorming exercises. Picture Plot and Tell-a-Tale introduce decision making, a step beyond brainstorming. When children know in advance that they will be making decisions based on their brainstorming, they tend to be more cautious and realistic in the ideas they generate—but they also are tempted to move prematurely toward making judgments before they have completed the brainstorming process. Again, this should be discouraged.

In addition to games, you can encourage your children to exercise their imagination in real-life situations. Parents, for example, can encourage children to brainstorm several possible solutions to conflicts, vacation time, or budget priorities. Teach them to look at every problem from more than one angle. Teachers can let their students brainstorm ideas for outside activities, class presentations, and answers to lesson questions.

Uses Muses

Hold up an object (such as a rock, rope, or fork). Tell everyone to write down as many uses for the object as he can think of. They are to do this in private, without talking to one another. (If your children can't write, have them think of answers to themselves.) Give a one- or two-minute time limit. Then bring them together again and tell them they will have one minute to tell you all the ways they can use the object. Every idea is worth one point to the group. No one is to say anything bad about any idea; if anyone does, the whole group loses five points. Let them brainstorm as a group for one minute, allowing them to speak spontaneously. Write items down as they speak. Repeat the activity with another object and challenge the children to increase their score.

Processing questions: Why did our score get higher each time we brainstormed? Did it help to have some time by yourselves to think of ideas before doing it as a group? Why? Why is it important to hold off on judgment until after we brainstorm? Suppose you and your friends are trying to think of something to do together one summer afternoon. What can you do to make sure you get a lot of good ideas?

Be sure that your children grasp two important rules: (1) let each person think about ideas by himself first, and (2) hold off on judgment until the group has run out of ideas.

You can make Uses Muses more interesting by having the children pretend they are shipwrecked on a desert island or stranded in the wilderness. All they have are the items you hold up in front of them. Or you can take a problem of a story character from a book or a home evening or Primary manual. After you have read through enough of the story for the children to understand the problem, let them brainstorm solutions. Then read the rest of the story. This is especially great for older children, who like to deal with "real" problems. Do this often in your lessons.

Making It Up

Most of us have played this game at one time or another; it should sound familiar to you. It is both enjoyable and creative. Try this on children over five years old. Explain to your children that you are going to start a story (or poem or song), and that they will take turns adding one sentence to the story. Start the story (for example, "Once upon a time there was a frog"). Point to a child at one end of the group. Give him a minute to think (the others will have time to think of their additions as others speak), then have him continue the story. Keep rotating around the group until the children begin to tire. Just before the last round, tell them to end the story.

Processing questions: What makes this game such fun? Did it get easier or harder to make something up when it was your turn? Why? Some people believe that groups can't do anything creative, that it's always better to do something by yourself. What do you think? Why?

One variation to this game is to assign each child a character to portray (perhaps from the Bible, the Book of Mormon, or early Church history). As each person adds to the story, he must insert his character into the plot. You can also have them improvise a skit as they act it out, or let them invent a game by brainstorming the rules. Or take a familiar song and have them substitute their own words into the chorus.

Picture Plot

This game works well with children of any age. Seat your children around a table or in a circle and tell them to choose a secretary. (If your children are too young to write comfortably, assign an assistant to write for them.) If you have more than six children, divide them into smaller groups. Provide newsprint and felt-tipped marker for the secretary. Show a magazine picture and tell the group to make up a story about the picture, recording *every* idea generated by everyone. *The group with the most story plots will be the winner.* If you only have one group, provide an incentive for each plot, such as a star or a sticker. Older children love award ribbons. You can designate how many plots they need to earn a first-place ribbon, second-place ribbon, and so on. Everyone in the group should receive the same award, as it is a group goal.

State the following rules: (1) There will be no criticism during the brainstorming period, (2) far-fetched ideas are encouraged because they may trigger even more ideas, and (3) many ideas are desirable. Tell the children to remain silent for two minutes and think about the picture individually (thirty seconds for younger children). Give them five to fifteen minutes to make up stories (younger children should have less time). At the end of the period, declare a winning group or give out awards to your lone group. Tell them that the ban on criticism is now over: They are now to evaluate their ideas and select the best one. After they have chosen their story, have someone tell it to you. For processing questions, see Uses Muses.

Here are a few more ideas: Give the children a picture from your lesson and have them guess what your lesson is about; give them several pictures and have them tie these together into the same plot; for younger children's lessons on nature, set a flower, rock, or stuffed animal in their circle and have them invent stories about that object.

Tell-a-Tale

Try this on six- to eight-year-olds. Number your children off by fives (or some other number—adjust the game to the number of children you have to work with). Tell each child with a number one to draw his favorite animal. Number twos draw favorite flowers,

threes draw birds, fours draw people, and fives draw a
food. Encourage each child to use his imagination;
then tell them to make their pictures. (The pictures
should be drawn on 8-by-12-inch poster paper with
string attached so they can hang around the neck.)

After the children have finished their pictures, tell
them to write stories about their pictures. The length
of their stories should depend on the children's ages,
anywhere from one sentence to a page. If they can't
write, have them think up stories silently. When
stories have been written, make sure each child has
his picture hanging from his neck. Gather your children together.

Divide the children into groups of five (or selected
number), making sure each group has one child with
an animal picture, one with a flower, one with a bird,
one with a person, and one with a food item. (A single
group can play this as well.) Assign each group a part
of the room and instruct them to make up a group
story with their pictures and prepare to present the
story to the others. They can change their original
stories. Emphasize that everybody's ideas must be
used in the story and that you will choose a "best"
group (or decide how good it is if you only have one
group).

After the children have been given enough time to
prepare, gather them and give them a chance to present their stories. When all the stories have been told,
give each child a questionnaire (see below) and tell
him to fill it out. Read each question and allow the children to write either yes or no in the blank. Tell them
that if the sentence is true to them they should write
yes. If not, they are to write no.

Our Story

1. ____ My picture had many colors in it.
2. ____ We had fun making up our story in my group.

3. ___ I had lots of stories I wanted to tell for my picture.
4. ___ My group told a good story.
5. ___ Part of my story was in our group story.
6. ___ I liked making up a story for my picture.
7. ___ It was fun to hear everybody's stories.
8. ___ My picture was used in our group story.
9. ___ Everybody in my group told his ideas.
10. ___ I want to make up more stories.

Gather the questionnaires and write the name of each group on a chalkboard (that is, Group 1, Group 2, and so on). Underneath each group name, record one point for every "yes" written by the group's members. The best group is the one with the most points. (If you have only one group, have a graduating award scale: so many "yes" answers means they get a first-place ribbon, and so on.)

Processing questions: The best group was the one that had lots of ideas, included everybody, and had lots of fun. Let's go through these questions and see why each one needed a "yes." (Review Our Story questionnaire: yes answers for numbers 1 and 3 prove they had many ideas; yeses on numbers 5, 8, and 9 prove they included everyone; yeses on numbers 2, 4, 6, 7, and 10 prove they enjoyed brainstorming together.) Why do we need lots of ideas when we work together on a project? Why do we need to have every single person give ideas?

Other materials besides crayons can be used to create pictures (e.g., construction paper, glue, fake fur, or wooden craft sticks). For small children too young to be comfortable writing the questionnaire, ask the questions verbally and have them place an X for no and 0 for yes in the spaces.

You can have older children draw their individual pictures around a lesson theme. For these older participants, use the following questionnaire, which is equivalent to the simpler version and can be processed with the same key.

Our Story

1. ＿＿ This is the first time I've drawn this particular object this way.
2. ＿＿ I feel that everyone in our group enjoyed making up our story.
3. ＿＿ I had several stories in mind for my picture, but had trouble deciding which one to write.
4. ＿＿ I believe we put together a good story.
5. ＿＿ Many of my ideas were put into our group story.
6. ＿＿ I enjoyed working on my story.
7. ＿＿ I enjoyed hearing what other people wrote for their pictures.
8. ＿＿ We put my picture into our story.
9. ＿＿ Every single person contributed to our group story.
10. ＿＿ I'd like to do this again sometime.

DECISION MAKING

The exercises in this section are essentially more brainstorming games extended by stages into decision making. Their basic elements are:
1. Brainstorming session
2. Narrowing of choices
3. Making a final decision

$100 Decision

This is a good mixed-age game. Give each child a sheet of paper and pencil. Have him write or draw everything he might buy with $100. (If they can't write, have them think about what they would buy.) Then reassemble the group and tell them to brainstorm for five minutes on things they can buy with $100. Brainstorming rules apply (see the previous section). Tell them to narrow their choices to five (or ten if they have brainstormed many items). Then have them write realistic prices next to each item. (If you have small children, go ahead and write your personal estimate, as they probably won't know how much things cost.) Have them decide how the money will be spent. Remind them that they only have $100 for the whole group.

Processing questions: Was it harder to decide what you wanted to buy for yourself or for everybody? Why? How are decisions we make together different from decisions we make by ourselves? How did you reach your final decision? We live in a democratic country. What does that mean? If we have a lot of decisions we have to make together, what kind of skills do we need to develop?

For older children, have them pretend they are Primary or Scout leaders of a ward or branch. They have only $100 (or any amount you think is appropriate) to buy supplies. Or they could be missionaries or pioneers buying supplies. Younger children could pretend that a friendly grocery story owner volunteered to donate candy for their next party, but he will give only one kind of candy. They must decide what kind of candy they want for their pretend party.

Group Goal

Tell your children to write or think of qualities that make a good class or family. Give them time to brainstorm alone. Then have them brainstorm as a group, while you write their ideas on a chalkboard or poster. Tell them to narrow their choices to five. After they narrow their choices, have them select the most important quality. Give them time to reflect, on their own, on ways the class or family can achieve that chosen quality. Have them brainstorm together again on ways to achieve their goal, narrow their choices to three strategies, then select a final approach. Get the group members to commit themselves to their chosen course.

Processing questions: Do you feel satisfied with your final decision? Why? What kinds of compromises did you have to make? Were there some ideas generated that you would not have thought of by yourself? Did this help you make a better decision? Suppose I had just told you what we were going to do: Would you feel like doing what I told you to do as much as you feel like doing what you have planned? When it comes to group goals, why is it important to talk things out like we did?

Spaceship Engineers

Let your eight- to eleven-year-olds blast off with this game! Pass out paper and pencils and tell your children to design spaceships on their own. After enough time, put them together and give them, as a group, three pieces of paper. Tell them to design three different spaceships, combining elements from all of their drawings. They may add new features if they want. After sufficient time, let them pick the best out of the three and explain why it was chosen. For processing questions, see $100 Decision and Group Goal.

Did your children enjoy this exercise? Let them do it again by having them design a Zion settlement, a Nephite ship, or a paradise garden.

PROBLEM SOLVING

So far we have been concentrating on isolated skills in peer relations. Once you feel that your youngsters enjoy each other and feel comfortable making decisions together, you can combine all these skills into problem-solving situations. It doesn't hurt to try one or two fantasy problems before launching into reality, particularly if your group has had problems completing tasks in the past. Fictional cases are dress rehearsals, a way of practicing leadership and caring behavior in a low-risk environment. This section will not only consolidate principles of loving relationships exercised in previous chapters, but will also introduce such organizational aids as delegation, accountability, and research. My personal experience has been that children between seven and eleven years of age benefit most from exercises in this section. I would not recommend them for children much younger than that, although younger children can be involved with older ones, as in a family.

A fantasy problem is basically a case study. We place the children in a make-believe problem and allow them to solve it on their own. The four cases suggested here are really only examples; you can create your own case to suit your unique lesson and personality. The following elements should help you guide your children through a fantasy case.

Believable case: The problem must contain some element of plausibility, something that adults would worry about if faced with the same dilemma. My favorite tactic is to plop my students into a historical context. Nephite Defense, Noah's Ark, and Traveling to Galilee are all time tunnels to practical problems that could or did happen in the past. Another way to make a situation believable is to place the children vicariously into an adult world of concerns. You can do this by forming them into miniature replicas of adult problem-solving groups such as the United Nations, a senate, a city council, a school board, or a bishopric. This is excellent training for solving problems that plague their own world.

Special interest roles: You may or may not want to assign roles and motives to each child. This means asking the child to assume the identity of a fictional or real character and to act with that character's special interest at heart. A Nephite would probably feel differently about some issues than a Lamanite, for example. I've tried both ways, and find that assigning roles makes the case more realistic and consequently promotes more lively discussion. On the other hand, allowing children to be themselves seems to help them work out their own style of relating with other young-sters. Each of the cases suggested here carries role assignments, which may or may not be used.

Formal leader: Every time you run a case study, choose a different formal leader. Take the time to re-view with your children the qualities needed in a leader and his supporters (see chapter 4). In addition to this review, provide your leader with a simple, written guideline (agenda). Most groups that experience frus-tration and failure in a task are not prepared or organized. You can help your children avoid failure by training them (especially formal leaders) to prepare a general plan ahead of time. They need to get used to following a written agenda. The agenda you provide should be tailored to your fantasy case, but here is a general prototype to follow:

1. Opening prayer
2. Review problem (read the case)
3. Define goal (What are we trying to accomplish)
4. Brainstorm solutions
5. Pick final solution
6. Closing prayer

Further inform your leader to regulate the atmos-phere of the group. He needs to be sure, for example, that everyone participates, that "rips" are discour-aged, that judgments are postponed during brain-storming sessions, and so on.

Noninterference in decision making: Though you may have to regulate the *process* (proper brainstorm-ing techniques, agenda setting, and so on), especially the first time, *never* interfere with the actual case. In other words, when the children look to you for an answer to a problem in their case, give the ball back immediately. Allow them to exercise their own imagi-nation and agency to creatively overcome the ob-stacles before them. Allow them to argue over how many armies to send over to Alma's Pass, how much space to give Noah's elephant, how much money to give to starving Africans. Don't be afraid of conflict: as long as no one is personally attacking another person, it's a healthy way to grind out solutions. If an argument degenerates into verbal abuse, I've found that I can cool it down by ringing a bell, pointing out what people said to each other that had nothing to do with the problem ("You're stupid" is a personal attack; "I think you're wrong because . . ." is all right), and making the guilty parties apologize to each other before allowing them to continue. Hot debates usually don't occur until the time comes for picking the final strategy, one of the last items on the agenda, and then only if you have succeeded in creating a truly believable case for your children. Pat yourself on the back when they become seriously involved with their fictional problem. The more noise the better!

The fourth exercise in this section, City Council, is a transition between fantasy and reality. Here we introduce delegation of responsibility, research, and accountability. This activity requires two group meetings far enough apart to allow for individual "homework."

You'll be pleasantly surprised at how serious the children's solutions will be and how thoughtfully they conduct themselves. You may even wish they were running some of the adult organizations you have been a part of! If you have a highly cohesive group by the time you reach this section, you will also be surprised at how quickly they accomplish the task you've given them. A group with good personal and organizational skills can cut meetings in half and accomplish three times as much as the average committee. This happens in any group, adult or child. Another phenomenon is hard to describe in words: You will feel an invisible bond drawing all of you closer together, a warm unity that only singleness of purpose can achieve. This feeling is much more pronounced and obvious when your children have actually accomplished something "for real" (see next chapter).

Nephite Defense

Many years ago a group of Lamanites repented of all the murders and robberies they had committed against the Nephites. They decided to join Christ's church and swore never to fight again. Every adult man broke his spear and arrows and made a covenant with God never to lift his arm in battle again. After they were blessed with forgiveness from Heavenly Father, they humbly asked the Nephites if they could settle among them. Though they were frightened, the Nephites took courage and allowed the converted Lamanites to build cities and farms on their borders. The new settlers began to call themselves Nephites too. The old Nephites were so joyful as they watched their new brothers living righteously that they decided to protect the converts by patrolling around the borders and catching any "bad" Lamanites who tried to come in and burn one of the new towns. Many years passed in peace and happiness.

Then the Lamanites in the desert grew angry at the new Nephites. They felt betrayed. They decided to march in war against the converted Lamanites and kill them all. They poured in through the Zarahemla Plains and murdered whole towns on the outskirts of the land. They began to invade through other mountain passes as well. The new Nephites refused to break their promise with God, and so they were killed mercilessly. The Nephites did not have enough scouts to fight these large Lamanite armies. They had to decide how many more men, if any, they would send out to defend their converted brethren. Many of the Nephite families did not want their sons and fathers to fight for somebody else.

You are a group of Nephite military generals in an emergency session. You have the accompanying map to work with. You must decide how many armies to bring in, where to send them, and what to do with them (such as have them guard, march offensively, and so on).

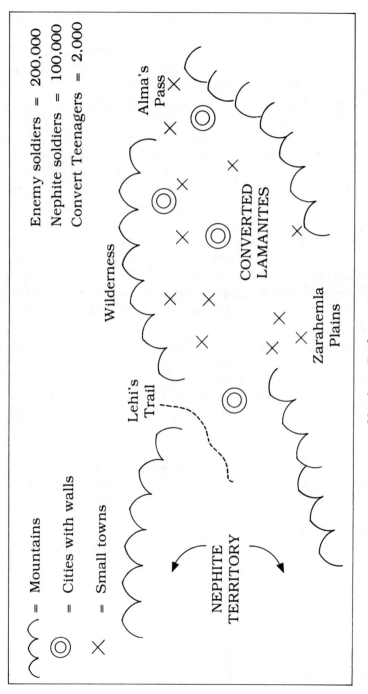

Nephite Defense Map

Enemy soldiers = 200,000
Nephite soldiers = 100,000
Convert Teenagers = 2,000

Alma's Pass

Wilderness

CONVERTED LAMANITES

Zarahemla Plains

Lehi's Trail

NEPHITE TERRITORY

〰 = Mountains
◎ = Cities with walls
✕ = Small towns

Helaman: You support the covenant which the converted Lamanites have made. But you also believe that the Nephites will not send an army unless the new settlers show some self-defense. You think you can persuade the new Nephites to let their teenage sons, who were too young to make the covenant years ago, march to war. You have great faith in God and you believe these boys can fight like men.

Amulek: You don't understand why the new converts don't stand up and fight for themselves. You think they might be too afraid or too religious; you're not certain which. You like to keep your men around old Nephite borders, protecting your own people. You're willing to see a few men go, but not the whole army. In any case, you don't want to send anyone unless the new settlers fight, too.

Zebul: You've been in charge of the roaming scouts patrolling the new settlements. You and your men have grown to love the converted Lamanites because of their great courage and faith. It wrings your heart out every time a village gets massacred. You want to save these people at any cost.

Corianor: You've been fighting Lamanites on a Nephite border far away from here. You don't know much about this situation. Your men respect and love you. They would follow you anywhere and die under your command for any reason. Because of this, you are very cautious. You'll keep an open mind and decide what you want to do after you've learned more from the other generals. You are very good at creating compromises during deadlocks.

Abinad: You hate meetings. Time means lost lives. You'd rather be out on the battlefield with your men somewhere. Your favorite strategy is to shorten the meeting by siding with somebody you agree with and pushing as hard as you can to get everybody else to stop "jawing" and start "jamming." You have a problem, though: Both Helaman and Amulek are good friends of yours. You admire both of them for their

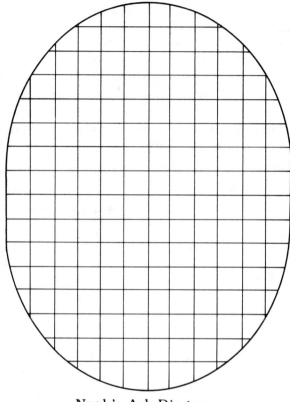

Noah's Ark Diagram

military genius. They seem to disagree with each other. You secretly decide to go with the general who seems to believe most strongly in what he is saying.

Noah's Ark

Noah has already completed the design of the top floors of his ark. But he feels an urgent need now to go out and preach repentance to his neighbors and warn them about the flood. He assigns you, his children, to lay out the bottom floor of the ark. You must decide where to put the remaining animals, how much space each pair of animals will have, and where your walkways will be. Refer to the diagram to see how much room you have to work with.

Walkways must be provided so you can feed and water the animals. They must be at least a square wide, and give you access to every cage. Below is a list of the animals Noah wants on the bottom floor. The numbers in the first column tell you how many squares each pair of animals needs to stay alive during the long voyage. The second column tells how many squares an animal pair needs to be strong and healthy, and the third shows how many squares you need if you want that animal couple to start having babies on the ark.

	Weak but alive	*Strong*	*Have babies*
Elephants	4	6	10
Lions	2	4	6
Deer	2	3	5
Sheep	1	3	5
Cows	2	4	6
Rabbits	½	1	1
Chickens	½	1	3
Goats	1	3	5
Bears	2	6	8
Elk	2	4	7

Japheth and Ham: You've been herding the family sheep, goats, and cows. You want to see your herds grow large again so the family will have something to eat and wear while the crops grow. You believe these are the most important animals for the family. On the other hand, you'd like to see the lions and bears die during the trip. You think it's stupid to bring along animals that will kill your flocks.

Shem: You're the hunter in the family. You believe deer and elk should multiply during the trip and get a head start. Not only will they provide meat for the family, but they will keep the lions and bears alive, too. If the family and God's plan for every creature to live on the earth are both going to make it, the deer and elk have got to be given first priority.

Japheth's wife and Shem's wife: You've been taking care of the rabbits and chickens. You believe these animals should be given all the space they need to have babies because:

1. Rabbits and chickens have lots of babies at the same time (bigger animals only have one a year).
2. The babies grow up fast (in three to four months). Chickens can start laying eggs and rabbits will be ready to eat while they are still on the trip.
3. The family can eat eggs and rabbit stew during the voyage and still have two of every animal when they finally land somewhere.

In other words, you believe the family gets more food value for the space.

Ham's wife: You have always loved the wild animals of the world. You feel they need a good head start because they won't have human beings to take care of them. The elephants, lions, deer, bears, and elk all need to be made healthy enough to survive in a world with very few living things left to eat. In fact, they should have babies while they can, so that if any die, there will be enough surviving to carry out God's plan of filling the world again with animals.

Traveling to Galilee

Jesus of Nazareth, the famous speaker and healer, is teaching by the Sea of Galilee. He will be there for only another week, however, before he retires to the wilderness for prayer. And where he will be next after that, no one knows. Refer to the map to decide your route from Jerusalem to Galilee. (If you decide not to use role assignments, add the following: You are taking a group of investigators from Jerusalem to hear Jesus, so that they may know he is the Son of God. You are worried about time, safety, and feelings. If you go straight through Samaria, your Jewish friends probably won't go because they hate Samaritans. It is

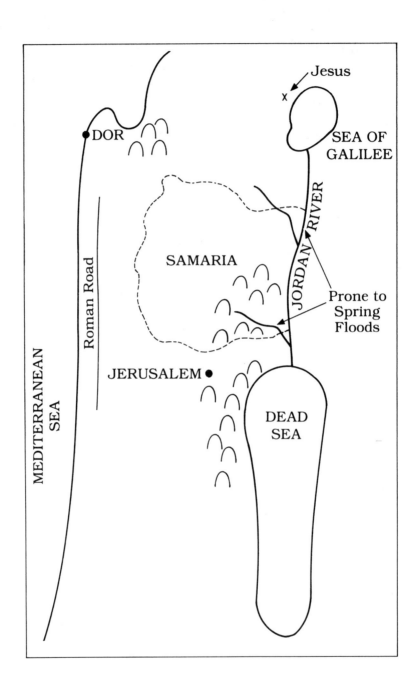

Map of Israel

spring, and if you go by way of the Jordan River, you are in danger of drowning in a flash flood. If you go clear around the west side of Samaria, it will take exactly one week to reach the Galilee, provided you aren't stopped by Roman soldiers and compelled to carry their gear for a day, which happens about half the time.)

Andrew: You are one of Jesus' Apostles. You have convinced a group of investigators from Jerusalem to travel with you to Galilee to hear Jesus. You want to get there in plenty of time to not only hear him, but talk with him and observe him for a few days. You are burning with a desire to get these people there as soon as you can. The fastest way, by far, is straight through Samaria. The Mediterranean coast is the least desirable route because it would only leave one extra day in Galilee.

Martha: You are going because your son, Jacob, is going. He threatened to get baptized if you didn't come along and listen to a strange man from Nazareth. You are a very orthodox Israelite. You absolutely refuse to have anything to do with gentiles, and especially Samaritans. You hate Samaritans, for they are evil, wicked heathen who mock the Jewish religion.

Jacob: You have a burning testimony of what Andrew has taught. The only reason you wouldn't let him baptize you is because of your mother, Martha. You are hoping she will be converted when she hears Jesus and spends enough time with him. She is stubborn, but very good in her heart. You have been inspired by Jesus' parable of the good Samaritan and how he stayed in a Samaritan village for two days to preach. You want to get to Galilee as fast as possible.

Abram: You are a friend of Jacob's. You are going because you like to see new places and you have never been to Galilee before. There's just one thing you feel strongly about: you are terrified by water. Sometimes you have nightmares about drowning in the sea or in a sudden flood coming from nowhere.

Elizabeth: You want to be baptized, but you don't feel worthy yet. You haven't seen your parents, who live in Dor, for years. Last time you saw them, you had a bad fight with them and left home leaving them in tears. Now that your father is dying of leprosy, you feel an urgent need to see them as soon as possible, to tell them that you are sorry and that you love them. You don't want to meet Jesus until you've made peace with your parents. You want to drop by Dor on the way to Galilee.

City Council

This is a transition exercise between fantasy and reality in group work. It requires a great deal of imaginative brainstorming, individual responsibility, and group cooperation. You will need two separate meetings for this activity. The agenda for the first meeting should be as follows:

1. Opening prayer.
2. Statement of goal: To help our community be a better place to live in.
3. Brainstorm community problems. (You can kick off the discussion with general categories and encourage the children to come up with more specific ideas. For example, you can suggest that they think of problems they noticed around the playground, classrooms, downtown, roads, danger areas, or with stray animals.)
4. Make a final selection of the problem. (Get them to choose one very specific problem. Make sure it is something they feel strongly about.)
5. Brainstorm solutions and resources. (Have them think of ways to solve the problem and places they can go to find out if such solutions will work, such as the library, the school principal, and so on.)
6. Delegate responsibility. (Make sure the formal leader understands that he must divide up

"homework" among everyone, including himself. In this case, each person needs to research a particular solution.) Provide the following checklist for what they will report on at the next meeting:

    a. Has this solution been suggested by anybody else?

    b. If so, what happened? Why?

    c. How much would this solution cost?

    d. Where would the money come from?

    e. Would the solution cause other problems? If so, what?

    f. Do you think this solution could work? Why?

(Talking to people seems to bring the greatest satisfaction to youngsters. Encourage them to talk to appropriate people who could answer their questions.)

    7. Closing prayer.

At the second meeting, which should be held about a week later, use the following agenda:

    1. Opening prayer.

    2. Restate the problem.

    3. Give reports. Each person should orally report on his homework.

    4. Choose a final solution.

    5. Draft a letter to an appropriate authority, proposing solution to problem. (I have never been disappointed by a senator. Senators have always answered our letters, and the thrill of it for children is joyful! If you can justify a letter to a senator by stretching the problem to fit his jurisdiction, you won't be disappointed by the result. This is a great way to give your youngsters a successful experience in community citizenship.)

    6. Closing prayer.

Note: Be sure to send the letter off for a quick reply.

6

Successful Goals:
"We Can Do It Together"

Children are capable of achieving great successes. A hundred years ago six-year-olds herded cattle, eight-year-olds hunted game, ten-year-olds helped provide for widowed mothers and many other siblings. But today we sometimes treat perfectly normal children as though they were mentally retarded. What a waste of opportunity! We assume that because adult commit-tees often get mired in muddy thinking and irresponsi-ble behavior, children would be doubly difficult to work with. In truth, they are much easier to deal with. They aren't caught up in complicated personality con-flicts, past experiences, bad habits, or complete role rigidity. I think I know why the Savior often took little ones in his arms after a dialogue with double-talking Sadducees. How refreshing to talk directly to a human being with no guile, whose open face radiates a lighted mind and a receptive heart! You can do just about any-thing with a group of children who love each other and you. Why not lead them to the top of a mountain—the edge of a star—the window of heaven itself? It is hard to give children challenges, because we like to see them passively happy all the time. Yet if they are to grow, expand, and experience an increase of joy, they must have challenges. This is an eternal law for all of God's children.

ACTIVITY PLANNING

You can give children opportunities to achieve goals together by having them plan their own parties, class presentations, service projects, vacations, summer programs, talent shows, or garden plots. You can initiate organized strategies to bring an inactive friend to church or bring happiness to a relative or lonely adult. Children can solve problems that concern them, such as litter in the neighborhood, an ugly playground, or lack of equipment. They can form "companies" and raise their own money by washing cars, selling punch, cleaning yards, writing computer programs, putting on neighborhood plays. The opportunities are endless.

When supervising the first "real" planning session, you can either preside as the formal leader or hand the whole thing over to one of the children. If they are familiar with simple rules for conducting planning sessions, such as they would learn from chapter 5, you will only need to be present as a resource. If they haven't been trained to feel comfortable with the rules, guide them through their first planning opportunity— then the next time simply remind the formal leader of the rules and step out.

The basic steps to planning an activity are simple and easy to remember. To review them here I will use an example from our ward, because it was a challenging yet highly successful experience. We decided to let four ten- and eleven-year-olds (one volunteer from each of the Blazer and Merrie Miss classes) plan and organize one of our quarterly Primary activity days. These activity days are difficult to plan because they have to appeal to seventy children between the ages of three and eleven, and still stay within a tight budget.

We felt that a child committee might work, however, because these particular children came from very supportive classes with healthy relationships between the students themselves and their teachers. It was a great opportunity for me to compare the performance of adult and child groups given the same task. We in the Primary presidency usually spent from four to six hours in planning sessions for each activity day. In addition, each of us would labor for five to ten hours on our own to complete our delegated tasks. The ten-year-old group spent an hour and a half planning the activity (forty-five minutes in each of two sessions) and from two to six hours each in individual effort. Yet their Primary activity was one of the most successful ever organized. It was a children's paradise of apple dunking, hot-dog picnic, sponge throw, fishing booth, treasure hunt, jelly-bean count, wooden-stick crafts, and candle making! How did they do it? Both the adults and the children knew the same planning principles—being very teachable, however, the children had enough faith to follow those guidelines. All we had to do as advisers was provide a very general outline, the same one you can use with any planning session with your children.

1. *Decide on a goal.* What are we trying to accomplish? Goals help to keep the group focused on the task. You can have the children decide what the goal is, or if the activity is Church-sponsored and already has a policy goal, take thirty seconds to write it on the board. In our case, the goal was to provide an enjoyable, positive experience that the whole Primary could share together.

2. *Brainstorm.* This particular group wasn't used to brainstorming together, so we provided an incentive for every idea generated (a quarter of a candy bar, which was group-shared—they lost a whole candy bar if anyone made a judgment). Review chapter 5 for brainstorming techniques. Our planning committee

came up with about thirty ideas, then narrowed them down to five.

3. Reach a final decision. Our group decided to combine their five remaining ideas into a "Country Day" and added other features to fit the theme.

4. Delegate responsibilities. Assign each child a portion of the activity to take charge of. It is always better to let them volunteer for a responsibility they want to have. They should be encouraged to involve other children on their subcommittees. This group certainly took this advice to heart. They enlisted a total of fifteen friends and eight adults to help them out on their assignments. So, even though individual work time was low compared to the Primary presidency's typical activity day load, the total in man-hours was very high. Provide a typed list or have them write the following items to report on at the next meeting:

a. Draw what your part will look like when it is done (physical design).

b. Describe step by step how it will work.

c. How many people will you need to help you *make* and *run* your section during the activity? Write down their names.

d. What materials do you need? How much will they cost?

e. What problems have you thought of?

5. Set a time and place for the next meeting. The follow-up meeting should be held within a week from your first session. We had a four-day interval. Scheduling it soon motivates group members to plunge into their assignments immediately, while enthusiasm is still high.

During the time interval between meetings, talk to your children and ask them if they need any help. These contacts remind them to complete their responsibilities and let them know you care about any problems they might be having. If you have a formal leader, communicate only with him. Encourage him to talk with everyone else in the group and report back to you. During our big activity planning, I called each of the children once a week until the activity. Though they never reported any major problems, they seemed glad to have someone to talk to about their progress.

During the second meeting, follow an agenda similar to the following:

1. *Give oral reports.* Let each person get up in front of the group and give a report on his assignment, following the guideline you provided at the last meeting. After he completes his report, ask questions and clarify any vague details. Encourage the other children to ask questions as well, so that problems can be unearthed and examined. In our activity day committee, for example, the girl who was in charge of the sponge toss seemed unsure as to how to go about building the board. As a group we brainstormed different ways to build the board, which gave her ideas for a completely different approach than any of us had thought of before. A boy in the group was vague about who would man his fishing booth. A few questions finally prompted him to write down the names of people he thought would help him. Don't be afraid to hash out details. The process trains your children to think of the details that turn ideas into reality; it gives them a sense of security knowing their project is thoroughly thought out; and finally, it makes them feel important to be treated as adults. They will treat their individual responsibilities the way you treat them as committee members.

2. *Tie up loose ends.* Once major aspects of the activity are ironed out, other details need to be discussed and delegated. Encourage committee members to brainstorm problems or details that hadn't been thought of before. In our case, we had to come up with an advertising campaign for "Country Day," design an overall layout for the recreation hall, and decide when to meet at the chapel to set up booths.

In summary, a two-session planning activity should follow the simple agenda outlines below:

First Meeting

1. Decide on a goal
2. Brainstorm
3. Reach a final decision
4. Delegate responsibilities
5. Arrange the next meeting

Second Meeting:

1. Give oral reports
2. Tie up loose ends

A final note: We need to recognize the achievements of our youngsters when they carry through on these group assignments. A word of thanks can go a long way toward future eagerness to participate in group challenges. The committee members for "Country Day" were awarded certificates of appreciation during the activity itself, where they also received applause and cheers from their friends.

How did "Country Day" materialize? I wasn't sure myself how it would turn out, for the task of entertaining seventy other children is an awesome task for ten-year-olds. Instead of seventy children, eighty showed up, the biggest Primary crowd in years. Two hours before the activity, the committee members showed up with ten other children to set up booths and decorate the hall. When the fair got under way, bewildered volunteer adults were carefully instructed by eleven-year-old supervisors on their responsibilities. It was a well-organized, enjoyable hour for everyone. It was the first time in my life I had ever been to a Primary activity where there wasn't a three-year-old crying somewhere, or a group of sulky nine-year-old boys sitting on the stage. Another victory for kid power!

Try it with your group of children. There's admittedly some suspense on your part until it's all over, but you'll be glad you gave them a chance to prove themselves.

By the time your children can responsibly achieve goals together, they will be united and bonded together with cords of love based on deep affection, mutual respect, and a thrilling sense of oneness and purpose. Step by step, with games and laughter, you can fulfill your greatest teaching assignment on earth: "Teach them to love one another."

Selected Bibliography

Bales, Robert F. *Interaction Process Analysis.* New York: Macmillan Publishing Co., 1975.

Beck, Steven; Forehand, Rex; Green, Kenneth; and Vosk, Barbara. "An Assessment of the Relationships Among Measures of Children's Social Competence and Children's Academic Achievement." *Child Development* 51 (December 1980): 1149–56.

Brilhart, John K. *Effective Group Discussion.* Dubuque, Iowa: WCB Company Publishers, 1982.

Brown, Jeannette A., and MacDougall, Mary Ann. "Simulated Social Skill Training for Elementary School Children." *Elementary School Guidance and Counseling* 6 (March 1972): 175–79.

Burstyn, J. N., and Feichtner, S. H. "Development of Individualistic Behaviors in the Classroom." *Journal of Experimental Education* 42 (Summer 1974): 12–17.

Haheman Medical College and Hospital and University of Pennsylvania Hospital, Research Report, 1971.

Hare, A. Paul. "Theories of Group Development and Categories for Interaction Analysis." *Small Group Behavior* 4 (August 1973): 259–304.

Heslin, Richard; Jones, John E.; and Pfeiffer, J. William. *Instrumentation in Human Relations Training.* San Diego, Cal.: University Associates, 1973.

Jones, John E., and Pfeiffer, J. William. *A Handbook of Structured Experiences for Human Relations Training.* Vols. I-VIII. San Diego, Cal.: University Associates, 1981.

Kagan, Spencer, and Knight, George P. "Development of Prosocial and Competitive Behaviors in Anglo-American and Mexican-American Children." *Child Development* 48 (December 1977): 1385–94.

Lewis, Michael D. "Self-Concept and Learning: Breaking the Vicious Circle." *Elementary School Guidance and Counseling* 2 (December 1967): 173.

Strain, Phillip S. "The Role of Peers in Modifying Classmates' Social Behavior: A Review." *Journal of Special Education* 10 (Winter 1976): 351–56.

Zeichner, Kenneth M. "The Development of an Instrument to Measure Group Membership in Elementary School Classrooms." *Journal of Experimental Education* 48 (Spring 1980): 237–44.

Index